Frederick Harrison grew up in Hull and joined the Merchant Navy when he was fifteen. His dream was to sail to America to buy a genuine pair of blue jeans. It was only when he confessed this to the galley boy, halfway across a heaving Atlantic, that he discovered he could have bought them in Leeds. Restored to dry land, he moved south and studied at the London School of Economics before becoming a lecturer and writer. His play, *A Hard Day's Night*, was performed by the Hull Truck Theatre Company in 1988 and has toured Britain and Germany. He lives in Brockley, South London, with a conglomeration of citywise cats.

FREDERICK HARRISON

Travelling Cat

Grafton
An Imprint of HarperCollins*Publishers*

Grafton
An Imprint of HarperCollins*Publishers*
77–85 Fulham Palace Road,
Hammersmith, London W6 8JB

Published by Grafton 1989
9 8 7 6 5 4 3

First published in Great Britain by
Souvenir Press Ltd 1988

ISBN 0 586 20694 9

Set in Times

Printed in Great Britain by
Scotprint, Musselburgh, Scotland

To John Course

Contents

1
Somewhere in a 'Fridge North of Watford

I suppose the saga really began early in 1987, one dark and windy night in the depths of winter, when most self-respecting cats appeared to be firmly nailed to the floor in front of the fire. Self-respect, however, was never high on Podey's list of priorities and the habits of a lifetime undeterred by the weather. Which was why I eventually found her by the side of the road on the edge of her territory and a good fifty yards from the house. Oddly flat, she was otherwise unmarked, with none of the usual paraphernalia of violent death doled out to the street ignorant in the area. Judging by the amazed expression on her face, death was sudden, unexpected, and probably inaudible given the recent onset of deafness from old age.

I stood over her, stunned. Podey, single parent of half the cats in Brockley; the one-night stand for generations of wandering toms. Every spring, even now, ancient battle-scarred lovers arrived to gaze nostalgically through the windows. I stared down unbelievingly. Podey had snuffed it.

I knelt down and prised her off the road, leaving a faint cartoon-like impression of her in the soft new tarmac. As I stood watching it fill with rain, impressions crowded in. Me and this banjo-shaped dead cat went back a long way. Memories of happier, more innocent days crowded in. Comparing bruises after the mock battles of Grosvenor Square. Smoking a first joint, and watching myself turn green in the mirror as Pink Floyd howled and tinkled through another (seemingly) nine-hour track. Willing myself to have a good time at the Isle of Wight concert along with one hundred thousand other cramped, sodden, knackered Bob Dylan fans: and in retrospect, succeeding. Arriving at the LSE in 1968 to find myself in a brief magical situation where people and politics were coming together with an intensity that marked for life many who took part. Who needs madeleine cakes when you have a dead cat on your hands? I had bought her in Hull during the last summer of the 'sixties. I was a second year at LSE. She was six weeks old.

Suddenly, unexpectedly, I began to cry. So much for my counselling course support group. Emotionally repressed, eh? 'Give yourself permission,' droned that Greek chorus. I immediately stopped crying. I trudged back to the house with Podey. I placed the flattened depository of a thousand memories on the kitchen table and sighed. For the next two hours I listened to scratchy rock and roll and watched mental television.

An instant replay of almost twenty years. With minute figures on fast forward, speeding into and out of relationships with jerky little unco-ordinated movements that would have seemed comical if the

Podey, single parent of half the cats in Brockley.

8

reality had not been so different. I watched us all compromise and subside and occasionally self-destruct. Watched us move with tiny steps from youth to early middle-age, guilty and grateful to let the idealism fade: blaming our loss of innocence and an indelible yearning for something lost on the government, bad relationships, wrong career decisions; even the threat of AIDS. It wasn't really us, we told ourselves; it was simply the times we were living through.

Whatever. Through it all sauntered old Banjo here: outraging the neighbours with her garrulous and highly public sex life; astounding friends with her voracious appetite; peeing genteelly down the plug-hole of the bath and generally ignoring life's imperatives to conform to anything. Suddenly it dawned. Tears started again. This mis-shape was an important part of my life. I made a decision.

*   *   *

'Stuffed and mounted?' said the cheerful voice at the Natural History Museum. 'Well, no, we don't do pets. But I know someone who does.' He did.

'Now then,' said the brisk Yorkshire voice of Graeham Teasdale, 'what was the condition of the animal when you found it?'

Condition? 'Well,' I whispered, 'dead.'

Mr Teasdale sighed. 'You have got it in the 'fridge?' he asked.

The 'fridge? 'Oh yes,' I lied.

'Should be all right then,' he said. 'Just one other thing. I've got a long waiting list, quite a few months. Some people ring me up very upset, and by the time I've got around to it, they're forgotten all about it.'

I looked at the compressed pet on the table. Suddenly I remembered those frisbee-shaped, wind-dried ducks in the window of Poon's Chinese restaurant. For no particular reason, half my life changes seemed to have started there.

'Not me,' I said.

A brief glance in the *Yellow Pages* and transport was decided upon. 'How much does the parcel weigh?' asked the voice from Roadline.

9

'About seven pounds, actually,' I speculated. How could a cat that ate so much stay so thin?

Guilt whispered by in the shape of a long-gone neighbour.

'And another thing. Have you seen the state a that poor cat?'

In came the Greek chorus, right on cue.

'How does it feel?' they crooned.

'It feels like sodding guilt!' I yelled back and to myself.

'By the way,' I said to Roadline, 'I think I should tell you. It's a cat.'

'Sorry,' said Roadline, 'I think Telecom's playing up again. I thought you said it was a cat.'

'Erm, it's a dead cat, actually.'

There was a brief silence on the other end of the line.

'You're quite sure it's dead, are you?' they asked carefully.

*   *   *

Two hours later they arrived. I opened the door to two large men and the kind of removal van they use to evacuate embassies.

'Did they tell you how big the parcel was?' I asked.

'Oh yes,' said the older one. 'They told us all about the parcel.' He made a curious noise, like a horse slowly breaking wind. His younger mate joined in with a heavy breathing sound you usually come across when the telephone rings late at night. It dawned on me they were both trying not to laugh.

'It's in the kitchen,' I said primly.

'In the kitchen,' repeated Heavy Breather, breathlessly. They entered. They stood looking down at the parcelled Podey wrapped in kitchen foil, brown paper and string.

'It looks like a banjo,' said Horse Fart. 'How come it's so flat?'

Without warning, all the accusations of my support group began to come true.

'Well,' I said, and then: I started to giggle.

'She-got-run-over,' I gasped.

'Splat,' sighed Heavy Breather, the bumps on his shaved head catching the light as it bobbed in suppressed laughter.

10

'I'm sorry,' I giggled, 'I don't know what's come over me.'

'Stuffed and mounted,' whinnied Horse Fart.

'She had forty-four kittens, you see,' I began, vaguely trying to retrieve some dignity.

'She probably won't notice a thing, then,' gasped Horse Fart.

'Unreconstructed,' intoned the chorus. I felt a twinge of guilt. I had, after all, once been on the Lewisham Equal Opportunities course. I was alert to incipient sexism.

'I'm really upset about this,' I began, with a total lack of conviction.

'Get two more,' said Heavy Breather.

'No. It wouldn't be the same,' I said.

'Then you can have three,' he said.

I was mystified.

'Then you can have three going up the wall. Like ducks.'

We stood around the kitchen, hanging on to various things, gasping for air. It says much for my emotional and overtired state that I thought he had a point.

Finally they left. Retribution was not long in following. Possibly because of Podey's spectacular sex life, several cats can be found lounging around outside the house at all hours. A week after her demise I was sitting by the front door surrounded by several of them, including the notorious Cheesy: a sort of scrofulous disposal unit with a smell that makes other cats' eyes water—hence the name. I used to think Cheesy was the nearest thing the species has yet achieved to a complete failure. Entirely indiscriminating in her sexual orientation—I once saw her try to mount a rabbit—she is permanently bad-tempered, has a call like a rusty hinge and eating habits so disgusting even hardened street toms turn away at meal times. If Podey was a last reminder of the 'sixties, Cheesy is a constant reminder of the 'eighties. Impervious to the stunned reaction whenever she appears, Cheesy's idea of ingratiation is not to bite you.

As I sat, ignored as usual, among the cats, two large dogs appeared. Normally dogs have the good sense to give our corner of

11

Cheesy: a sort of scrofulous disposal unit with a smell that makes other cats' eyes water.

the square a wide berth. And cats are not usually known to have mob instincts. But a tradition has grown up among my mob that when dogs threaten, the collective approach is much the most effective. So far. These particular dogs belonged to the squatters down the road and would eat anything. Wild rumours had circulated from time to time. Cheesy, having just hoovered her way through a large mound of food, was unusually slow on the uptake. Normally she led the mob into battle. Not this time. Before the cats could react, the dogs were among them.

I suppose with hindsight I should take it as a compliment that all five cats—even Cheesy—instinctively saw me as a sanctuary. Whatever the motives, I suddenly found myself draped with fear-inflated cats. As the snapping dogs whirled, I gave my first public exhibition of break dancing. A small crowd began to gather, as they invariably do in Brockley when blood flows. Advice was given.

'Kick 'em in the bollocks!' yelled the fearsome Red Janet, social worker.

'Mind the pussies!' trilled an animal lover.

Street theatre is clearly at a premium in Brockley. It can be no coincidence that the immortal Marcel Stein, he who earns a living hammering nails up his nose, lives locally. Suddenly the dogs got bored, retreated and were gone. I began to extract the cats one by one. The last was Cheesy. As I held her by the scruff of her scrofulous neck, Animal Lover piped up again.

'They don't like being held that way, you know.'

I was getting really pissed off.

'Look,' I said, 'they're brought up to it. Their mothers do it all the time when they're kittens. Right?'

I reached out to reassure Cheesy and prove my point. One stone of infuriated cat sank its teeth through my finger. Whaaaaaaa!

The small crowd, which was beginning to break up, reassembled at the sight of fresh blood.

'I told you they didn't like it,' commented Animal Lover smugly. Cheesy hung on, teeth embedded, cross-eyed with the effort.

'Get this frigging cat off me, you great ponce!' I yelled, offending two of Brockley's three minority action groups—the third are the police—in one sentence. Blood continued to flow, as did the advice. Cheesy's eyes took on an ominous glazed look. I remembered a recent documentary on piranha. I tried persuasion. Even as I spoke, it sounded ludicrous.

'Here, Cheesy. Nice Cheesy.' There was a muffled growl. I tried straight abuse.

'Ger off! Yeh scrag bag!' The growl went up an octave. I had an idea. 'Rattle the food bowl!' I shouted desperately.

Animal Lover picked up the aluminium food bowl and banged it. The sound had an immediate effect. Several cats, oblivious to the confusion, appeared from nowhere. Cheesy hung on. Animal Lover banged again. The assembling cats mewed hopefully.

13

Normally dogs have the good sense to give our corner of the square a wide berth, but these particular dogs belonged to the squatters down the road and would eat anything.

'Food! Yeh daft prat!' I yelled at Cheesy. She uncrossed her eyes and swivelled them balefully over the warbling throng. A brief atavistic struggle between basic instincts ensued. Greed won. Cheesy opened her gory mouth and fell to earth. As I tottered off, blood-stained and perforated, to join the throng at the local GP, I passed a group of punks from the squat.

''Bout time you got some street cred,' sniggered Rat Scabies unsteadily.

I am not a superstitious person, but sometimes the evidence of circumstances beyond our control persuades. A week after consigning Podey to a deep freeze and the future attentions of a taxidermist, I had found myself providing an *al fresco* snack for Cheesy. Naturally I became infected and spent five miserable days on antibiotics. The day I finished the course Cheesy was hit by a car. Unscathed, she retaliated by biting a tyre. She was returned, her nose—broken long ago—covered in shredded rubber, by three admiring members of the local SPG patrol. It was obviously a slack night.

That evening Cheesy lay marinating in front of the fire. She rolled over, belched and went to sleep. Outside, a police car yelped its way to one or another of Brockley's more popular bloodsports. I closed the curtains on the night. In the stillness of the room, was it just my imagination, or could I hear a peculiar creaking sound, like old ice moving? Could it be that somewhere, in a 'fridge north of Watford, an ancient, deep-frozen cat was laughing? I looked at Cheesy, true heir to Podey, asleep and entirely at ease with the fractious world of the late 'eighties. With the benefit of hindsight, I should have taken the events as an omen of things to come.

Cats know things people don't.

2
Catastrophe

It was officially the first day of spring when I had the idea. Naturally, gales of sleet were scything across the deserted streets as I walked back from the restaurant where my newly ex-wife and I had just celebrated our Decree Absolute. 'If we'd put as much effort into making the marriage work as we have the divorce,' she'd said drily, 'we might still have a marriage.' She had a point. Ah well. At least we were still friends. Looking around at the misery other people had caused each other while splitting up, it was no mean achievement.

Anyway. While walking home, the idea struck. At 15 I'd joined the Merchant Navy for two years, and never lost the habit of travel. It was time to move on for a while, whispered the idea that had clearly found its time. Only: I was still feeling a bit delicate from the parting of the ways and, although living alone was showing increasing dividends, travelling alone was not yet appealing. On the other hand, I was hardly in the mood for a casual travel companion. Arriving home, I ploughed through the usual safari park of miniatures surrounding the entrance to the house and—the penny dropped. Why not take a cat?

This immediately raised another problem. Which one? Given the familiar throng lounging around the front door like an LA street gang, the choice at least was plentiful. On the other hand, I would be sharing space, the very confined space, of a Ford Transit. That immediately eliminated ninety per cent of the choice. After all, sharing space with a raddled streetwise gangster who thinks washing is for cissies, and spraying every conceivable surface a sacred macho duty, could cause problems. For the cat, that is.

Eventually I narrowed the field down to a shortlist of three. The first, Cheesy, might come as a surprise. But recently she had

17

Cheesy might seem an unlikely candidate, but recently she had mellowed. Like an old boxer, she commanded respect, admiration and some caution.

mellowed. This was possibly due to brain damage caused by running head first into stationary objects in the belief that they, like most people and all cats, would move out of the way. As with an old boxer, she commanded respect, admiration, and some caution.

Unfortunately she blew her chances when an old friend, an American writer, came to visit for the first time in several years. In the way of old and particularly American friends, we soon fell into a deep discussion of the meaning of life and our respective roles in the scheme of things. We were interrupted by a low and prolonged hiss. My friend stopped in mid-sentence.

'Do your cats have a neurotic trigger when their space is invaded?' she asked.

'Erm . . . they vary, actually,' I hedged.

'It's just that the one under the table is pissing on my feet,' she said.

So much for Cheesy's travel plans.

That left Wally and Pugwash; given that immortal Bonzo had passed on due to kidney failure and that his mother, Podey, awaited collection, stuffed and mounted, somewhere north of Watford. Wally is rather like Bonzo in some ways. A born survivor: impervious to life's slings and arrows and incurably optimistic. Except that Bonzo had only three legs. One hind leg had been removed after a fight with one of his brothers over the right to mate with their mother, the incorrigible and now eternally stuffed Podey. I tell you, Greek mythology has nothing on a cat's domestic life.

Unperturbed by suddenly becoming a triped, Bonzo continued to lead an active life to such an extent that few realised he actually had a disability. 'That was Bonzo,' I would say to visitors, sitting by the front door on a summer evening, as the Flying Tripod, one hind leg blurring up and down like a demented piston, zoomed by.

'He has only three legs,' I'd say casually as old Blurred Bum disappeared in a cloud of dust. Bonzo was just one of many cats I've known who developed a genius for stopping conversation. His favourite gambit was to sit on the wall at the front of the house and, cocking his head at an angle in the time-honoured way of all cats when scratching an ear with a hind leg, wave his stump in the air. In the end I lost count of the horrified strangers who knocked on the door with the same blanched expression.

'Excuse me,' they'd whisper, 'but I think your cat's lost a leg.'

Don't tell me cats have no sense of humour.

I find it hard to describe Wally, and almost everybody else has the same problem. He is quite simply the ugliest cat I have ever seen: a sort of Elephant Man of the cat world. One eye is actually lower than the other and both look in different directions. At the same time his two left legs are unaccountably shorter than his two right legs. This presents no problems for Wally but tends to disorientate the casual observer. As he trots towards you, he appears to drift to one side. The eye naturally follows the motion and you expect him to arrive at a spot about two feet to the left. Suddenly, you find one of Britain's ugliest cats in front of you. Some people take days to recover.

Of course, Wally has no idea he is ugly and indeed he has a very sweet nature. A test of moral fibre is to stroke him. Few pass the test, including me. For that reason, I decided to leave Wally at home. That left Pugwash.

Pugwash is a son of Cheesy. That in itself should be an automatic disqualification. In fact, like many an offspring of an eccentric parent, Pugwash is the opposite of his fearsome mother in the same way that Hippies bred Punks. Except that in this case it's the other way round. Pugwash actually sniffs flowers and is the only cat I know who leans against walls. He is not an over-achiever.

To be fair to the nature-nurture debate, he was virtually raised, with infinite care and patience, by Monica in her weaving studio upstairs. As a result he is quite the friendliest, most laid-back cat in the neighbourhood. A people groupie, one stroke and he's anybody's. And he's house trained. The perfect travelling companion, then.

Some time later, protesting urban cat and owner climbed into the old Ford Transit and hit the road heading south and west for unknown destinations.

Pugwash was in a sulk. He was, after all, entirely urban. 'Say goodbye to the city,' I said unnecessarily to the back of his head as we travelled through the endless conurbation of brick and stained concrete. 'From now on, my man,' I said, 'we're living by the days.'

Pugwash, leaning against the inside of the cat basket, sniffed and stared stolidly ahead.

At last we hit the open road, even if it was a motorway. I wound down the window and took a deep breath. We were heading down the M3 and bound for Wiltshire. I let out an involuntary yell of release and looked down at Pugwash. He was staring up at me and had a familiar faraway look in his eyes. There was the sound of a low, prolonged hiss. Oh no! Nature was overcoming nurture.

Pugwash was making his protest.

(Opposite) *Wally: a sort of Elephant Man of the cat world. He has no idea that he is ugly and indeed has a very sweet nature. Pugwash: quite the friendliest, most laid-back cat in the neighbourhood, one stroke and he's anybody's.*

3
Sex and the Single Rabbit

Arriving on the top of the old Drove Road with my reluctant travelling companion, there was a sense of relief in more ways than one as I climbed out of the driving seat. I looked accusingly at Pugwash who was still asleep on a side cushion amid the fumes of his earlier protest. Oh well, I could always aerosol the van later. It was evening and clear, and the rolling hills of Wiltshire stretched off into the blue horizon. Aah, freedom.

Along the Drove Road and into the distance, rabbits were bouncing up and down as if it were a giant trampoline. I brought out Pugwash who, leaning against a fence post, sat in a trance watching his first rabbits. Memories revived.

It was pointed out to me recently that I seem to have had a rather chequered career with domestic animals. Note the term. Calling them pets would be rather like calling Adolf Hitler a house painter. This was certainly true of the two rabbits I maintained during the late 'sixties in a manner to which they were clearly unaccustomed.

The first was called Flopsy Bunny. Yes, all right. It was 1969 and London was full of daft prats in paisley calling each other Bilbo. As it turned out, it probably was the most inappropriate name ever given to a rabbit. I was informed too late that only female rabbits burrow. This turned out to be true. But there are rabbits and there are rabbits. Flopsy turned out to be a compulsive excavator with homicidal tendencies.

'Where did we go wrong?' I said to co-owner Pauline one day, as once again I got out the Dettol after a brief but unsuccessful skirmish to save the rose bed.

'Maybe if we mated her it might take her mind off things,' she said wisely.

I looked accusingly at Pugwash sitting amid the fumes of his earlier protest.

23

Why not? I thought. After all, it works with everybody else I know. And besides, the garden, which now looked like some corner forever England in a foreign field after a particularly heavy pasting, was clearly on its last legs.

Flopsy was a medium-sized Dutch rabbit. There was a a time when I equated the Dutch with peaceful co-existence. Not any more. I discovered that the only rabbit in the area available for nuptials was owned by friends a few doors away. He was called Gareth. In retrospect, it was unfortunate he was a dwarf.

Come the big day and a small group of us gathered by the lawn—not on it, since it was by now a no-go area due to the tunnelling. We let Gareth loose and he sat nibbling the wreckage of a geranium.

'Flopsy,' we all trilled. 'Florpsy!'

Eventually the ferocious mud-covered head of the rabbit appeared with a familiar mad gleam in her eyes. And then, a miracle. Flopsy saw Gareth and shot out of the hole as if from a cannon. With one bound, as they say, she was by his side. Or rather (gasp) crouched down submissively in front of him. Gareth seemed to expand with macho pride and then—bonk. It was over so fast, one blink and it would have been missed. And that apparently is what happened. Gareth missed. Or to be more precise, he fell off.

Undeterred he remounted, there was another blur of action, and bonk, he was off again.

'Maybe if I held him steady?' I said, instantly regretting the offer. This was not the first—or last—time my liberal humanistic tendencies resulted in me making a total prat of myself. Tenderly I held Gareth over Flopsy. Brmmmmmmm. The speed was un-believable. At last the rites were concluded.

Several weeks later, Flopsy busily piled hay in the corner of her new hutch and pulled fur off her chest. And then, one day, there they were. Seven bald, blind little bundles of infant rabbit. Ahhh. I felt the swell of paternal pride by proxy. Not for long. The next day the hutch was empty. Flopsy had eaten them. It was back to trench warfare.

Ah well. Other times, other places. And other rabbits. In 1967 I was living in Hull and the sexual revolution had arrived with a bang, so to speak; particularly if you were a teenager who had just left the sporadic purdah of two years in the Merchant Navy.

The rabbit was known as Oh What!. Readers entering early menopause may remember this as a catch-all retort to almost anything that happened when all the world was new.

'D'you want some brown rice, man?'—'Oh What!'

'Erm, I think the house is burning down, man.'—'Oh What!'

At that time I lived in the top floor flat of a house on Spring Bank which had a gambling club—Club 49—in the basement. Next door's basement contained an antique shop, and the parties the owner used to run were later to put Hull on the map in Gay society.

The back gardens of the two houses ran together and the outdoor May Balls held by the Gay fraternity every year for themselves and the gambling fraternity were wondrous to behold. Long after I'd gone to bed, enthusiastic renderings of 'We are the Vaseleenees! Little girls and boys!' sung to the tune of the Ovaltine song by huge hairy dockers in frocks, floated up from the garden. Spring had duly arrived on Spring Bank.

It was into this colourful scene that Oh What! entered. Somehow it seemed entirely appropriate that I should keep a rabbit. Food was no problem. Oh What! consumed anything, from leftovers to the carpet. Exercise was also solved by opening the window and putting him/her out on the roof for a run. Oh What!'s favourite recreation was television, as it was for the numerous mice sharing the top floor. 'They're attracted by the UHF signals,' said a prosaic friend. I reckoned they were infatuated with Nyree Dawn Porter, along with everybody else at that time. It says much for my state of mind then that it seemed perfectly reasonable to sit watching *The Forsyte Saga* with a carpet-eating rabbit and a row of besotted mice.

The night of Hull's First Drug Bust, I was in bed with a girlfriend called Fritzy Lou Lou—no, really—enthusiastically exploring the parameters of the sexual revolution, when there was a hammering at the flat door. Otherwise engaged, it failed to register at first. Then a

loud voice floated up the stairs. 'Open up. Police.' Obviously a wind-up by friends living elsewhere in the rabbit warren of the Spring Bank Collective.

'Open up. Or the door goes in!'

'Sod off, you rotten buggers,' I yelled back.

CRASH! In came the flat door and suddenly the place was two deep in large men wearing blue.

'Don't move,' said the enthusiastic police inspector. There was no answer to that one.

Afterwards I discovered that the girls in the flat below had acquired new boyfriends who just happened to be on the run from a (very) open prison. Doing time for dealing in cannabis. It so happened both houses were clean. This did not deter the Gung Ho inspector. It was after all very new and a first for Hull's police force.

Still naked, I was made to bend over as the police formed an interested half-circle and the inspector produced a little torch. Looking between my legs, I saw Fritzy with a sheet wrapped round her, trying hard not to giggle.

'It's not funny,' I said indistinctly. 'This is an infringement of my basic liberties.' It is not easy to be dignified when your head is upside down.

'It's not that,' spluttered Fritzy. 'It's just that I had no idea you had such a spotty bum,' she managed, before subsiding into hysterical giggles.

The inspector ploughed on. 'And this,' he said, directing his little torch, 'this is the most common of the male bodily cavities for secreting illegal substances in an emergency.'

What the hell, I thought. 'If you find any money,' I said, 'it's mine.'

Just at this crucial moment Oh What! made an appearance, hopping in through the window off the roof.

'Excuse me, sir,' said an alert young constable, 'a rabbit's just come in through the window.'

'And I'm not bloody surprised,' snarled the inspector.

(Opposite) He sat in a trance watching his first rabbits.

Back on the old Drove Road, it was almost dark. I considered the journey from Spring Bank to the here and now, and the twenty years in between. In the east a huge full moon lit the road in that shadowless, slightly sinister way of moonlight.

'Bed,' I said to the still motionless Pugwash. I leaned over. 'I said—bed, Cloth Ears.' Nothing.

Pugwash was fast asleep, pursuing his own memories.

On the old Drove Road, it was almost dark.

4
Darling Buds of May

I used to think May Day was an affirmation of political convictions. I'm sure it used to be; although I suppose mass rallies in
honour of the Profit Motive might be a bit thin on the ground. North
of Watford, they might be.

In rural areas, things are a little different. At least, they were in the
part of Wiltshire where I now found myself: an enclave of retired
civil servants, armed forces personnel, Sloane Ranger weekenders,
ancient and not so ancient families, and a raft of local peons to keep
the whole thing afloat. Naturally, in such an environment, political
convictions have a walk-on part and the cut and thrust of political
debate has been subsumed into the transcendent and frequently
brutal culture of the WI, jumble sales, local gossip and, of course,
Morris Dancing. Which brings me back to May Day and the local
celebrations in the village of Ansty.

Ansty was the nearest village to the old Drove Road, where I was
ensconced in the Ford Transit with one (still) very urban cat. A
picture-book village of mainly thatched cottages arranged tastefully
around the medieval duck pond of the Old Manor House, it can best
be summed up by the following entry in the May Day programme:
'Ansty has been inhabited from very early days. The Tisbury and
Chilmark quarries were famous, but Ansty's were not.' Quite.

However, Ansty does have a very big May Pole. 'Perhaps the
tallest in England,' read the legend modestly. And May Poles, as I
discovered, can bring out the worst in people.

The May Day festivities began at 6.30 on a wet and windy Friday
evening. Gathered around the huge May Pole was a small crowd of
Barboured, green-wellied locals. Leader of the pack was a large,
impressive middle-aged woman wearing hairy tweeds, the aforesaid

29

One (still) very urban cat.

green wellies, several rows of pearls, and a camouflage flak jacket.

Approaching from the Drove Road, I assumed the festivities included a Tannoy. They did, but that was not what I was hearing. What I heard was the spine-chilling *basso profundo* of Ansty's leader, exhorting local schoolchildren to go through their paces around the May Pole. In a voice like a ruptured moose, and with that massive confidence born of many generations of unopposed eccentricity, she directed the proceedings around the May Pole as she probably directed most things in the village: with bizarre efficiency and iron control.

The children from Chilmark school danced prettily around the

May Pole and shyly took a bow at the end; then to be swept away and have their goose pimples wrapped in warm sweaters by equally chilled parents. The Moose retired to the nearby local—wittily named The Maypole—probably to down a few yards of ale and consume a side of beef. Meanwhile the May Queen's procession began from the old Crusaders' Hospice—now a semi-derelict garage—on the other side of the duck pond. Led by the White Horse Morris Men, a sweet-faced kid of 13 had been crowned with a small wreath of flowers—'for the second year running,' announced the actual Tannoy, and a dark ripple of muttering spread through the crowd like a stone dropped in the duck pond.

With the arrival of the Morris Men, all in white and waving white hankies as they danced to avoid the puddles, the main business of the evening began. That is, the murderously competitive enactment of spring by the White Horse Morris Men and the Dorset Triumph Folk Dancers—motto, we do it with bells on.

The White Horse men pranced energetically in formation. Large, mainly bearded, clearly out of condition, and not one a day over 40, they went through a lively routine with sticks, cracking them fiercely

The arrival of the Morris Men, all in white and waving white hankies as they danced to avoid the puddles.

together above each other's heads in a staccato of sound. It was all very macho, very impressive, and I wondered how they managed to miss each other's fingers, given that several dancers had their eyes closed in apparent ecstasy. In fact, they didn't always miss, as occasional agonised yells and muffled curses indicated. Accordions wheezed, bells jangled, and the whiplash crack of the sticks echoed back from the steep sides of Ansty's little valley, providing an appropriate background to the cries of pain. One must indeed suffer for one's art. Eventually the Morris Dancing finished and, white hankies clutched gamely between fingers rapidly turning blue, the White Horse men pranced in formation towards the pub.

'An' now!' announced the Tannoy, 'the Dorset Triumph Folk Dancers.' And so it came to pass that a group of large men dressed in shag rugs, green tights, and all wearing straw hats, appeared mysteriously by the May Pole. According to the Tannoy, the Dorset Triumph team was 'famous all over Europe in Dorset'. And indeed, they were—as the Tannoy announced several times to the mounting fury of the White Horse men—on their way that very night to France to perform in a festival.

The leader of the group stepped forward and made a little speech about the significance of May Day and its deep roots in English cultural history. The May Pole was apparently a male. I looked up at the huge phallic pole thrusting aggressively against the murky, overcast sky and wondered what a female May Pole looked like.

The first dance was announced: 'Jenny Plucks Pears'. I suddenly developed a wheezing cough as a solemn line of shag rugs stepped delicately through the puddles in tight formation. They were joined by The Maidens, in full green skirts, flowered bodices, and haloes of rapidly disintegrating flowers. Given that no one would see 30 again, I was impressed by the ability of the group to suspend disbelief among the crowd.

The dance concluded and the group pranced delicately off to one side. There was a silence, and then a wave of applause swept through the crowd. For whatever reasons, Dorset had triumphed. Sour-faced and muttering, Wiltshire White Horse men were emerging

The Maidens. I was impressed by the ability of the group to suspend disbelief among the crowd.

from the pub as once again the Tannoy announced the Dorset team's impending visit to France.

Encouraged by all this, Dorset Triumph moved into what became the highlight of the evening. A man without a shag rug, but wearing a hand-made bush of berries and flowers on his head, moved forward and crouched, foetus-like, in front of the May Pole. Another man, wearing the now familiar shag rug and glasses, leaped forward dramatically over the coyly prone Bush. Weaving as sensuous a circle as a short-sighted fourteen-stone man can, Earth Spirit—for it was he—whirled around the Bush until eventually . . . Of course! The birth of spring was being enacted before our very eyes. The deeply strange symbolic enactment of Spring Awakening by two large bearded men continued. The Bush began to rise—and this was particularly moving—slowly, haltingly at first, and then with more and more vigour. In fact he pranced around so energetically that his Bush fell off, but, undeterred, Spring sprang about the May Pole to the immense satisfaction of those members of the crowd not yet in the pub.

The dance finished to wild applause and as the White Horse men moved in ominously on the partisan Tannoy—which once again had announced Triumph's impending trip to France—the remnants of the crowd began to break up. And then, like some inexorable force of nature, Moose bounded out of the pub. Trailing people after her like iron filings behind a magnet, she made for the May Pole. 'Everybody! Dance! Dance around the May Pole!' she commanded. And who could not obey? Not me. Men, women and children, all of us joined hands, and soon the entire crowd was whirling around the huge pole, now draped with flowers and coloured ribbons, in a dance which had suddenly stopped being *ersatz*.

As the shouts and laughter of the crowd echoed off the steep sides of the valley and across the village, it became something else. Something much older and genuine. Spring had arrived in Ansty.

5
Fly Wars

We had been up on the old Drove Road for a while now, my faithful travelling companion and I. Given the choice between the wild untrammelled outdoors and the front seat of the van, Pugwash never hesitated. Which is why there was a brief scuffle every morning before said cat got the old heave-ho into the surrounding landscape.

Making adjustments to each other was all part of the game. Like friends or lovers going on holiday for the first time, we had had to adjust to each other's idiosyncrasies. This can result in fraught times. I once knew a couple who travelled all the way to Crete and within two days were refusing to speak to each other; would not in fact inhabit the same beach. And all because the poor woman began to hum whenever she became sexually aroused. Another couple I knew got on famously, in spite of the tendency of the guy to clean his ears out at dinner with a matchstick. Of course, in both cases, there may have been rather more to it than that.

In the case of my travelling companion, things were tolerably good—for the time being. Given that the nights were often still chilly, I had become resigned to Pugwash warming his great feet on me at all hours. Otherwise, his domestic habits remained unchanged: sleeping, eating, and the occasional enforced bout of violent exercise. In other words, his urban way of life remained unchanged; along with many other things, presumably, judging by the polls or, if I had been superstitious, omens such as unusual weather and bizarre phenomena such as Norman Tebbit smiling. All of which, particularly the latter, made me grateful for the relative isolation of the Drove

(Opposite) *Given the choice between the wild, untrammelled outdoors and the front seat of the van, Pugwash never hesitated—which was why there was a brief scuffle every morning before said cat got the old heave-ho.*

Road; up and away from the electoral battles of the plains. Besides, as I was to discover, I had my own wars to fight.

Thinking about the fate of urban lifers after the General Election of June 11, reminded me that I am not rural. By that I mean that the rules and regulations, the customs and rituals which govern country life remain elusive and strange. This was certainly true of the part of Wiltshire through which I was travelling: like the past, it was a whole different ball game; they did things differently here.

It was probably urban sentimentality, but the weather, animals, and insects apparently presented no problems for the locals. Meanwhile fields were getting hoed, crops fertilised, and animals fed, all in the mechanical, soulless way of modern agriculture. In the distance toy tractors trundled across the vast hedgeless fields as if driven by clockwork, creating delicate patterns of lines and sworls on a chemical earth that would not have disgraced a Zen garden. Indeed, watching the land being worked was like seeing the inside of a huge clock in motion; each part knowing exactly when to move or not in response to the automatic tick of the season.

Back on the old Drove Road in the old Ford Transit, things were a little different. Take one morning's breakfast, for instance. Now my breakfast was usually a simple meal: a couple of eggs, the odd sausage, nothing particularly complicated—or healthy, for that matter. The cooker was situated at the rear of the van, which meant that, with both rear doors open, I could actually stand outside and cook.

This had a strange effect on me. Atavistic memories of untried hunting skills rose to the surface as I boldly poked holes in the sausages to stop them exploding, or cracked open an egg. I was, after all, only a hundred yards from a Neolithic burial mound. The surrounding chalk downs—no, I don't know why they call the tops of hills downs either—had been settled for thousands of years and the land, now virtually denuded of trees by profit margins, was a favourite hunting ground of royalty for hundreds of years.

Impaling another sausage I imagined myself—despite a personal lack of interest in horses and dogs—astride a horse, lost in the thrill

36

Breakfast was usually a simple meal. Atavistic memories of untried hunting skills rose to the surface as I cracked open an egg.

of the chase, responding to the ancient call of the blood. I looked down at my faithful hunting hound . . . who yawned, scratched, and leaned against·the rear tyre waiting for any leftovers. Yes, I could always rely on my travelling companion to bring me back to earth.

With the casual skill of a born hunter I cracked another egg into the pan, and noticed a large black insect—some kind of fly—buzzing around my head.

'The price you pay for living by your wits off the land,' I said to Pugwash. The insect was joined by a second, and then a third. And then I noticed a faint drone, like faraway aircraft. I vaguely remembered a documentary about some dingbat who crossed aggressive honey-producing bees with lazy non-producing bees and ended up with homicidal honeyless bees.

The drone got louder and suddenly I found myself at the centre of a black whirlpool of insects. Bloody hell!

'Don't panic!' I yelled to Pugwash, panicking, and immediately receiving a mouthful of flies. My faithful travelling companion meanwhile was seated about thirty feet away, looking on with interest. Three seconds later I'd joined him.

I looked back at the black noisy cloud now circling the rear door of the van. I considered tactics and remembered my heritage. Retreat was out of the question: would Boadicea have backed away from a gang of flies? I ran round to the front of the van and grabbed a towel from the cab. Wrapping it around my head and face with just a slit left for the eyes, I returned to the fray, arms rotating like windmills, to rescue breakfast.

Absorbed in Fly Wars, I failed to notice the approach of a rider with two dogs running ahead. The crowd of flies started to thin out, and I cackled triumphantly.

'Take that! And that!' I yelled through the towel, arms still whirling. I was definitely winning. And then, about five feet above me, a voice drawled casually: 'G' morning.'

I peered up at this elegant vision which sat poised on his horse looking down at me. Have you noticed that people on horses always look faintly supercilious? The flies had almost gone now, just the odd straggler.

'I think the sausages are starting to burn,' drawled Equus man.

'Shit,' I exclaimed indistinctly through the towel.

'Sorry?' he enquired politely.

I unwound the towel from my head. 'Flies,' I said.

'Ah yes, flies,' he replied.

There was a brief silence between us which mirrored the ancient incomprehension of a man on a horse for a man who is on foot.

'Well,' he said finally, 'must be orf. *Bon appetit.*'

Effortlessly he turned his horse and rode off down the Drove Road, preceded by his two dogs running ahead diligently in the time-

(Opposite) I gazed up the old Drove Road at the burial mound silhouetted against the sky.

honoured way of faithful hunting hounds. My own faithful companion appeared from under the van, where he'd diligently scarpered when the dogs first appeared.

'You great useless idle Wozzek!' I yelled.

Pugwash, immune to insults from long exposure, proceeded to give himself a good wash while I raged on. After a while, the embarrassment subsided. I considered the charcoaled sausages framing the congealed eggs in the pan. *Nouvelle Cuisine* it was not.

I gazed up the Drove Road at the burial mound silhouetted against the sky. I would have liked to think that life was simpler in those days, in spite of all the evidence to the contrary. A world at least free of AIDS, pollution, nuclear devastation, and the threat of yet another Conservative Government. One thing was certain. They sure as hell found it easier to hunt breakfast.

6
Heathcliff Rides Again

Something strange was going on around me. Pugwash had changed. During the day he was the usual indolent slob of himself. But once the sun went down, he would slide Dracula-like through the van's side window and was gone; returning at intervals throughout the night with an array of small and very dead animals.

The first night this happened, I woke in the morning to find a neat row of corpses on the pillow. Eye-balling a stiffened rodent first thing is—I can guarantee this—a sure-fire way of getting anybody up in the morning. After I'd untangled myself from the van roof and had a good rant at a mildly bemused cat, I realised it was done with the best of intentions. The carnage was clearly intended as a top-up to the food supply—and a discreet recognition of my hunting skills. It was hardly Dracula's fault I didn't fancy Dormouse Tartare.

Probably as a personal response to the General Election results, I found the regeneration of the cat's hunting skills reassuring and a more realistic balance of instinct and learned response than I was used to from the mangy army of reprobates back in Brockley. And it was certainly a healthier balance than our species seems to have achieved for itself.

I suppose an appreciation of balance and harmony is bound to occur once anybody gets away from the kicked-over ant heaps of the cities for a while. Particularly when summer is sweeping through the countryside like a wave. It all seemed so orderly, like a computer with just one tried and tested floppy disc. New green and blossom had exploded on cue; brilliant yellow squares of ironically named rape broke up the standard green of other crops; and birds everywhere

(Opposite) Pugwash had changed. During the day he was the usual indolent slob of himself, but once the sun went down . . .

had stopped bonking and were busily yelling territorial warnings to each other as they kept house. In that respect, at least, it was not unlike the neighbourhood back home in Brockley.

There was, of course, another side to all this natural order and balance stuff. Conformism. And the iron laws of nature sometimes looked as insubstantial as a party manifesto beside the diktats of what was respectable and acceptable and what was not in this corner of Wiltshire—or Wessex, as the Tourist Board will have it.

Just outside the village where I had parked was a small, immaculate, quaint, but genuine gypsy encampment. At that moment it was occupied by a younger member of the family. Other members were on the road for the summer, but the son, along with his young wife, had stayed behind for the sake of the new baby. The family, I was told, were well known and well respected in the area. They had acquired an enviable range of country skills and were known to be good with horses—an important plus in an area where four-legged friends sometimes take precedence over the two-legged variety. And the father—as everybody pointed out—was in the army.

The quietness, the romantic but sanitised image of the camp site, the genuine skills that appealed particularly to would-be country people, all these things contributed to the family's role in the area as the acceptable face of nonconformism. And that can be a delicate business, as I discovered when talking idly to a quartet of upmarket newly-minted locals.

The two men stood discussing the local farmers' mistakes with crop rotation, in the same confident and knowledgeable way that they once ran government departments and that London yuppies criticise unemployed Northerners. And then: an approaching clatter announced the arrival on the scene of The Bare-Back Mounted Young Gypsy. The young man stopped to make polite conversation and the effect on the two women was electrifying. It was as if he'd been marinated in pheromones.

Suddenly I had the feeling we were in Mills and Boon land. The Gypsy had more than a passing resemblance to the young Olivier in

A small, immaculate, quaint, but genuine gypsy encampment.

Wuthering Heights and both women immediately went into what I believe ornithologists call a Sexual Display—much to the dismay of their two cardiganed, pipe-smoking husbands. The two wives moved energetically from one foot to another, twittered innocently ambiguous comments about the skills and sensitivity required for bare-back riding, and constantly adjusted their plumage—in this instance, loose perms, well-cut tweed skirts, and sensible jewellery for country wear.

In any social situation there are unsaid but important things. If not, generations of novelists and playwrights are heading for the knacker's yard. In this case, the air was suddenly full of unspoken thoughts from unrequited—and very generous—bosoms in the best traditions of the romantic novel. The effect on the two husbands was equally galvanising. They were suddenly reduced from Masters of All They Surveyed to uneasy, puzzled and—as they soon revealed—resentful Also-Rans.

Eventually the young gypsy made his polite excuses and rode on, the eyes of the women at least following him to the bend in the road.

43

The husbands consoled each other with a ferocious attack on the consequences of EEC milk quotas for the West Country.

What this little explosion of sexual chemistry pointed up, of course, was the ambiguity of conformism and the delicate balance any nonconformist has to maintain in such a rural community. The gypsy family were the acceptable face of nonconformism in the area for just as long as they conformed to what was acceptable. And making pegs, living in picturesque caravans, and possessing genuine rural skills that were in short supply were what was acceptable. Possessing the natural sexual energy of an attractive young man was clearly not. At least, not to half the population.

The unacceptable face of nonconformity could be found increasingly in the area as 21 June and the Summer Solstice loomed large. Small groups of multicoloured ramshackle buses, ambulances, and vans—of which I was temporarily one—were congregating surreptitiously after the batterings of the previous two years. This ragged army of dreamers and drifters was a logical response to the unemployment regulations, and to some horrified local burghers it appeared to be entirely anarchic. It was not, and maintained its own rigid laws on conformity. God help, for example, the Soho fashion disciple with Filofax extant who wandered inadvertently into the encampment of feral punks and prematurely aged flower children.

Conformity in this part of the country, then, was as complex an affair as I imagine it is elsewhere. I was reminded of another of its consequences in a local pub. In one corner sat a wrinkled, leathery ancient, looking like something found in a peat bog. Above him was a picture—a rather murky oil painting—of himself sitting in the same corner of the pub.

''E's bin coming in 'ere for over fifty years,' said the slightly younger barmaid. 'Never missed a day. Famous.'

I looked at this living fossil, preserved and mounted in the corner every evening by decades of routine and rigid conformity. I briefly wondered how anybody could become such a creature of habit. And then I thought of London Bridge in the rush hour. Like the hunting instincts of Pugwash, perhaps, it was not so strange.

Small groups of multicoloured ramshackle buses, ambulances, and vans—of which I was temporarily one.

7
Inside Outsider

High summer had arrived in Wiltshire. It was a term that had been given a fairly literal interpretation by some of my temporary travelling companions of late to while away the rain-sodden days. Still, as from the previous weekend it was now downhill all the way to 21 December. Given that some celebration was in order, and in spite of a police presence that had been more Hobbes than Hobbit, the new age travellers had been—and still were—determined to celebrate the English summer in their own inimitable way. Age may bring wisdom and restraint, but when it comes to sheer exuberant optimism, youth is dealt all the best cards. Take the previous week, for instance.

Speaking as someone who believes that each generation has the inalienable right to make a right prat of itself (didn't you?) in the process of establishing its own identity, I joined the wandering tribes near Stonehenge with a relatively open mind. And some unease. Like everybody else these days, I am not immune to adverse publicity.

Stopping to give a lift to a small group of spectacularly grimy teenagers in carefully arranged multicoloured tatters, the conversation immediately turned to Pugwash—basking in the new-found attention—and reincarnation. It was soon decided that Pugs had had a good Karma in his previous existence and, given his laid-back style—he was leaning casually against a ferocious looking Mad Max 2 clone at the time—he was bound on the upward path to enlightenment. They had not, of course, seen him dismembering several live mice that morning. A diplomatic silence was maintained regarding my own chances in the next life.

Arriving at Devil's Ditch camp outside Shipton Bellinger, we

It was decided that Pugs had had a good Karma in his previous existence and was bound on the upward path to enlightenment.

came to the wood where several dozen—and very soon several hundred—travellers were camping in preparation for the Summer Solstice.

Now my own memories of camping tend to be dominated by scratchy green jerseys, woggles, badges for rubbing sticks together, and sitting around in a circle chanting 'Aka-la! Dib dib dib! Dob dob dob!'

Akala was invariably tall and skinny in voluminous shorts; with a prominent Adam's apple and the voice of a failed accountant. I never did make the Scouts, by the way. I was hastily withdrawn by my mother after nice Mr Shaw, the scoutmaster, took camping out too literally and got four years.

Akala, I remember, was sometimes accompanied by Brown Owl, a woman of indeterminate age with legs like blocked drainpipes and a voice that rattled windows. The emphasis, I remember, was on personal hygiene, woodcraft and a healthy mind in a healthy body. Oh yes, and love of our English heritage.

Things were a little different back at Devil's Ditch. First impressions were likely to send Baden Powell turning in his grave so fast he could have powered a small town. Small tents and mini-benders were scattered throughout the wood. Not one was in line. The natural gloom of the wood was deepened by the smoke from innumerable small wood fires: some of it green wood, judging by the amount of smoke, so no Woodcraft badge.

Given that everybody looked like a refugee from World War Three, personal hygiene also needed to be worked on. Bodily functions, incidentally, were attended to in a manner as discreet and mysterious as astronauts'. People just drifted off into distant bushes and returned relieved. So was I when I realised how many people were camping in the wood.

On the other hand, quite a few had walked from London and then trudged the highways and byways of Wiltshire for a week under the provisions of the new Public Order Act. And most of them would walk the sixteen-mile round trip to the Stones that Saturday night so

First impressions were likely to send Baden Powell turning in his grave—no Woodcraft badge here.

full marks for fitness. And love of our English heritage? Well, more of that later.

First impressions, then, were not very promising. They were also very misleading. Take Angus, for instance: known as Fist to all his friends. Fist was every mother's nightmare. Encrusted with dirt; his spindly frame layered in coloured rags, his feet encased in huge boots; he topped it all with a large head brutally cropped except for a pony tail sticking out of the back of it, and a clenched fist tattooed on top. That and the ring through his nose completed the picture of a lad determined to offend.

Which was of course the object of the exercise. On a good day, he looked like a voracious stick insect on speed: and this was not a good day.

When he moved in on me with a baleful look, I began to look around for exits. Wrong. Within a few minutes I had been given a warm, funny and very perceptive view of the camp and his friends. It was made clear to me that the camp had 'good spirit': a fact often referred to with satisfaction.

By Saturday I had come to realise that if you peeled away the mystical connotations beloved of the travellers the underlying picture was one of a teenage heaven. A place where you could stay up and lie in for as long as you wanted. Where you washed if you wanted to and no one complained if you didn't, and where you could play loud music all day long because the only 'house' rules were the ones you made yourselves.

And there was the added buzz of challenging authority in what you and all your friends considered was a just cause. No wonder Wiltshire found them unstoppable. What teenager in their right mind could resist such a place?

But to stick a label 'hippy' on them was misleading. They were very different from their namesakes of the 'sixties, with that tough resilience very much a product of the 'eighties. The shared ragbag of beliefs, the mixture of Eastern philosophies and Celtic mythology, might have been handed down by menopausal flower children but they went their own way.

49

Much of the older generation was noticeably absent from Devil's Ditch camp, along with the multicoloured buses and vans. Old hippies don't die. They fade away at Glastonbury.

I left Devil's Ditch with some regret and joined the press bus in Amersham—my *entrée* to Stonehenge and the Druids' celebration of the Summer Solstice. And now, gentle readers, I can reveal what negotiators call a hidden agenda. Not a lot of people know this, but my paternal grandfather was a Druid.

Now to be a Druid in the twentieth century is to invite comment, as many discovered that Sunday when performing intricate and mysterious rites within a stony circle of emotional, overtired and frozen journalists. But to be a Druid in Hull—and be the only one—borders on the perverse.

Grandad kept the faith until the bitter end. My grandmother seized the opportunity to demand separate bedrooms—always difficult in a one-bedroom house—and with hindsight perhaps grandad, too, had a hidden agenda.

Arriving at Stonehenge in the pre-dawn dark, I stood in the now privileged enclosure of the site and watched large numbers of police pen in the rag, tag, and bobtailed army from Devil's Ditch. Every one had walked the eight miles in the middle of the night to celebrate the Solstice.

In the pre-dawn half-light a column of 22 Druids swept onto the scene like a nuns' chorus in the wrong opera. It could have been a reaction to Devil's Ditch, but every one of them looked so clean! Sadly, like a bad play watched by an indifferent audience, the performers—perhaps not surprisingly—just went through the motions. Sad because the remarkable site and a perfect dawn provided an extraordinary setting for a ceremony that might have been grand opera; instead of merely a circus.

But at precisely 5.02, as the sun rose above the horizon and over the mist-filled hollows below the site, and the first rays struck the Heel Stone, it was impossible not to want to believe that something significant was happening: if not for long.

As a Druid pulled out his collapsible horn to sound the arrival of

I stood in the now privileged enclosure of the site and watched large numbers of police pen in the rag, tag and bobtailed army from Devil's Ditch.

midsummer with all its magical, historical and sometimes daft connotations, English Heritage, official custodians of our English heritage, performed the *coup de grâce* on the proceedings it had already ruined, by flying in a helicopter at deafeningly close quarters to take publicity shots of an eccentric but endearing ceremony that had now become a charade.

In a sad little speech after the ceremony, the chief Druid, David Croxley, said: 'There are people inside who should be outside. And there are people outside who should be inside.'

It could almost be an epitaph for the 'eighties.

8
Walking with a Walkman

When you enter the countryside, you might reasonably expect to leave the city behind. But old habits die hard and with them the fantasies they breed. And it was the urban habits in particular that I had hauled along with me—and Pugs—to Wiltshire. Pugs, of course, had made a more successful transition from the urban to the rural. In fact, I had the sneaky feeling that if I did a runner, he would not only survive but thrive.

My own future would, I thought, be less certain. Adjusting from the daily knockabout farce of inner city Brockley to the deeply strange peace and quiet of Wiltshire was an ongoing process, as they say. Given the blessed Margaret's recent conversion to inner city concern—to lose one constituency is unfortunate, to lose several looks like carelessness—I was reminded that daily life in Brockley required a healthy set of survival tactics. Not all of them were suitable for daily life in Wiltshire.

Urban paranoia, for instance. Now in Brockley this was an invaluable asset. Always check out the shadows; cross the road when three or more youths approach; keep your eyes at street level at all times—virtually all things above seven feet can be ignored unless they're on roller skates and carrying a ghetto blaster; and never, never talk to strangers.

In the depths of the countryside, urban paranoia can sometimes result in what I believe psychologists call an inappropriate response. It took some time to curb the habit of sidling silently and watchfully past bemused locals I met on little country roads. I just naturally assumed their cheery 'marning!' had an ulterior motive. In Brockley, it would be the sure sign of a psychopath. I also had to shake the habit of peering suspiciously around trees and bushes all the time. For those of you about to enter the countryside for the first time, the place is full of them and it takes an age otherwise to walk anywhere.

On the other hand, I seemed to miss the most unlikely things. Noise, for instance. In the more isolated stopovers, I actually got withdrawal symptoms. I must have been the only person in Wiltshire who welcomed low-flying aircraft. The distant hum of traffic on some faraway motorway gave me acute pangs of nostalgia, and even a nearby passing tractor could lift the spirits.

This tendency confused fellow refugees from the front line, particularly other walkers. Which was why, when they came across me in plimsolls and an 'Ambiguity Confuses Me' T-shirt, cruising down some path singing along with the blissful noise of Prince or Smoky Robinson pounding from the Walkman, I was greeted by a slightly stunned silence. At least I thought I was.

Incidentally, I never have understood the need to dress up for the

Pugs had made a more successful transition from the urban to the rural than I had.

occasion. For me walking is simply a question of putting one foot in front of the other and not falling over. I also tend to have very simple tastes in clothes. Jeans, T-shirts, anything, really, that makes it difficult for locals to track me down. Not so The Walkers. Even in July—and they may be right—they come prepared for all eventualities, from blizzards to floods. Expensive boots, long woolly socks, anoraks, dinky little haversacks, and those inevitable woolly hats with bobbles on top that all seem to come from the same shop somewhere near Grimsby.

Still, I did sympathise with their confusion when they encountered me. I confused myself. 'Why,' I asked Pugs, 'if I'm concerned to turn my back on the cities for a while, do I insist on blotting out the sounds of silence at every opportunity?'

Pugs wisely ignored this key question of the late twentieth century and continued to examine his bum.

All these urban habits paled into insignificance, however, when set against my terminal addiction to English Soaps. Sophisticated friends—well, friends, anyway—argue that the popularity of many of these programmes is based upon a single myth: a caring, supporting community in an age of alienation. Maybe. All I know is that I slid into acute withdrawal whenever the battery ran down on my little portable TV. It was a tendency which was not always appreciated out in the wilds of Wessex.

Take one particular evening. It was warm and sunny, and I'd discovered a path off a small road with panoramic views of Dorset to the west under a sky that belonged on a Mother's Day card. It was also time for *EastEnders* and I might just as well have been blind, deaf and dumb as far as Mother Nature was concerned. Perched on the edge of my deckchair outside the van, watching the pasts of Dot and Ethel unfold, I was oblivious to all else. Apparently Ethel put it about a bit during the war (cor!) while poor old Dot's future sex life was blighted when she caught her parents bonking (blimey!). Meanwhile . . .

Just at the critical moment, when Ethel appeared to have died, a voice like a strangled hernia spoke behind me. 'I said, is this the way to Cranbourne Chase?'

I turned, briefly. A small group of walkers in full regalia stood a few yards away, the leader and speaker glaring down at me. 'What? Erm, yeah. Probably,' I said, turning back. Dot was leaning over to check Ethel's breathing (gasp!).

'Well, is it or not?' asked an irritated voice. Dot pulled back from Ethel and gave a wail. 'Oh, Ethel!' (Oh no!)

'Excuse me!' said the Hernia.

'Yes! Cranbourne Chase! Over there!' I snapped. Addictions do terrible things to people. Dot was heading for the door, panicking. I glanced at the walkers. With the exception of Hernia, they had drifted into a half-circle around the back of the deckchair, eyes glued to the screen. Suddenly Ethel opened her eyes. The half-circle and me drew in collective breaths. Bloodee hell! Even Hernia was silenced as the ancient friendship of Dot and Ethel was revived before our very eyes.

Eventually the familiar theme tune wafted across the idyllic rural scene and we all visibly relaxed: except Hernia, of course.

'Where are you walking to?' I asked conversationally.

'Cranbourne Chase!' he yelped. 'You said it was that way,' he added accusingly.

'Did I? Nooo. It's in the opposite direction,' I said.

'Thank you,' he snapped, and as I reached to switch off the TV, followed it with: 'Oh please don't let us interrupt your viewing.' As he flounced ahead of the now shamefaced little group he said to no one in particular: 'I don't know why some people come to the countryside, I really don't.'

He had a point. As I watched them stride off into the distance, the little bobbles on their woolly hats swinging in unison, I thought about the last few months of travelling around this part of Wiltshire. And I thought that I was probably not alone in projecting my urban fantasies on to the surrounding countryside. Not just the walkers, but the day trippers who drive all the way from London, then sit in the car admiring the view through the windscreen of protective glass. Or the retired couples who snap up their dream

The Divine Rachel, Earth Mother of the Chalke Valley.

thatched cottage at eighty thousand plus and then wonder why the days are so long as they settle into the awesomely boring routine of life in a dead village, killed by the voracious appetite of their own fantasy for the good life and all that entails. Including, and what a sad irony this is, the atavistic need to belong to a community.

Sad because the fantasy of a living, vital, supportive community, of the kind that glues millions to the television versions, really does exist in some parts of rural Wiltshire. In the Chalke Valley area of Cranbourne Chase, for example, is a local community as vitally alive and dramatically complex as anything dreamed up by the production

56

team of a Soap. Irony again, though: pubs feature at the centre of the community and indeed double as community centres now the old traditional centres have atrophied away. At Alvediston it's the Weight For Age Inn (a horse racing term), and at Ebbesbourne Wake it's The Horseshoe. Both are run by charismatic characters who would give Den and Angie a run for their money and who have turned their establishments into magnets for the local community. Particularly the Divine Rachel, Earth Mother of the Chalke Valley at Weight For Age.

It's possible that the Chalke Valley, and certainly some of its pubs, are the exceptions to the rule. But as I drove through the area for the last time, I came into Tisbury. A double wedding of two sisters was taking place. A large crowd of women had gathered by the church entrance, and the graveyard was crammed with the three families and friends. As I looked at the swirling, colourful mass of excited locals wearing those curious clothes that only get worn at weddings, I was reminded that all fantasies have some roots in reality. And if many rural communities are now merely geriatric dormitories or yuppie bolt-holes, there still seem to be enough real-live ones to feed the urban fantasy of a rural community that perhaps never was.

That said, I would miss the area and its rolling downs and some splendid characters. Pugwash would, of course, miss the dormice. Driving up the M3 I turned down the stereo cassette. 'Well, my man,' I said to the prostrate cat (he hates motorways), 'time to head for the coast.' Pugwash sighed.

'The sun, the sand, the sea!' Pugwash yawned.

'And the fish,' I said pointedly. 'Lots of lovely fresh fish.' His ears perked up like little pyramids. One thing about long-time travelling companions: they really get to know each other's weaknesses.

(Overleaf) *A double wedding of two sisters was taking place.*

9
Seacat

'That,' I said to the mesmerised and previously land-locked Pugwash, 'is the sea.' It was late evening and we were sitting on the beach at Walberswick. Behind us was a day spent in a Southwold that travel brochures probably featured thirty years ago and will do again if the nostalgia boom for the 'fifties continues.

It was not the day I was thinking about, though, as I sat by one stunned cat watching the miniature surf breaking on the beach. When I was fifteen I'd impulsively joined the Merchant Navy. Beatlemania had swept through Hull like a wave, and with that perfect logic all teenagers are blessed with, I was desperate to visit America.

I was supposed to stay on for 'O' levels and the headmaster was not amused. 'You want to go to America to buy some blue jeans?' he repeated incredulously.

'Yeah,' I muttered. How could an old man of forty understand the driving needs of a fifteen-year-old? Besides, I was in the middle of my bi-weekly sullen phase, not to mention a particularly virulent outbreak of spots. Having tried flattery, the headmaster resorted to abuse. His parting shot haunted my teens, as it was meant to. 'Fat and loud, son, is no way to go through life,' he said as the door closed forever on school and childhood.

Four days later I was heaving my insides out over the leeward side of the *Marengo* as we pounded through the house-high waves of a raging North Atlantic gale somewhere off Rockall. Looking at the calm, placid waters of the Suffolk coast, it was hard to believe this was the same element. In fact, given that my sole sea-going experience prior to the *Marengo* was the ferry across the Humber, it was hard to believe at the time.

As yet another great wave crashed solid green into the foredeck, the bosun appeared, strolling along a deck that seemed to be going in three directions at once with an infuriating ease. 'Get forrard wi' the others and secure them oil drums on the foredeck,' he yelled above the storm. The foredeck? Another great wave rolled along the length of it. I heaved breakfast over the side.

'And if anything small and round comes up,' he said, ambling off, 'hang on to it. It's your ring.'

'I don't wear one,' I trilled, mystified.

Minutes later I was giving a fair imitation of a human cork as one wave after another swept the foredeck. The rest of the crew seemed welded to the deck while waist-high water swirled around them and they worked to secure the drums. As I drifted by them upside down for the third time, the bosun wearily reached out and turned me the right way up. 'Go an' mek some tea, yeh silly little sod,' he mouthed, inaudible above the watery inferno.

Back at Walberswick all was calm. 'The sea is a fickle mistress,' I said to Pugs, who eyed me vaguely as presumably he tried to solve the eternal mystery of the constantly collapsing little wall of water a few yards away. This first day by the sea had reminded me of an old belief of mine: that something odd happens to the British when they

One stunned cat watching the miniature surf breaking on the beach.

come into contact with the sea. We are, I suppose, an island race and something three fathoms deep is touched whenever we get within paddling distance of it.

In the meantime, on this part of the Suffolk coast, time seemed to have passed by. Southwold and Walberswick are separated by a river. One a small town, the latter a village, both seem set in an aspic of nostalgia for an English seaside holiday that passed away two decades ago everywhere else. Walking down the High Street in Southwold gave me the shivers: the kind you get from the emotional confusion of *déjà vu*. Cut off from the arterial A12 by several miles of winding road—as are all the coastal places in this part of Suffolk—the town had the disarming look of an Ealing comedy.

At any moment I expected to see Cecil Parker bluster his way out of the menswear shop with the immaculate 'fifties façade. Or Terry Thomas caddishly chat up the fashionable young woman in the 'fifties-style outfit before he roared off in his perennial Morgan. By the time I got to the first bookshop I was convinced I'd find the wonderfully lugubrious Alistair Sim behind the counter, or perhaps Margaret Rutherford wobbling her many chins. Whatever: it was all so English, so genteel. And so middle class.

If the High Street was peopled with genteel ghosts, then it was fun to think of the tubercular wraith of Eric Blair roaming among them. and even more fun to think of him returning here from his down and out escapades in Paris and London in 1930, to metamorphose into George Orwell, England's finest scourge of the middle classes.

By the 'fifties, of course, the fishing village of Walberswick was a favourite resort of left-wing intellectuals in general and stalwarts of the Fabian Society in particular. And as they reeled happily out of The Bell pub after a ferocious evening of converting the world to socialism, and returned to their renovated prole cottages, they continued with innocent irony the English tradition of middle-class intellectuals mapping out the future of the working classes while comfortably ensuring their own. Meanwhile, a few miles down the coast at Aldeburgh, a real revolution was taking place as a certain B. Britten proceeded to grab English music by the scruff of its neck and

Southwold: the town had the disarming look of an Ealing comedy.

drag it kicking and screaming into the second half of the twentieth century.

And then something seems not to have happened. That wave of energy of the mid-'fifties passed on and a second wave that, among many other things, swept me to America in the 'sixties, passed Southwold and Walberswick by. The area always was a favourite place of retirement for the Civil Service, even in Orwell's day. And perhaps that's why Southwold appears to exist now in a time warp. Almost everyone seems to be middle-aged or older, although, unlike the retirement villages of Wiltshire, the town does have a life—albeit one gently paced to the needs of most of its inhabitants. A pace that, frankly, could seriously damage your health if you lived there and happened to be less than middle-aged in mind and body.

Back on the beach at Walberswick, Pugs was suspiciously prodding some old seaweed. After a day in the Southwold time capsule, and stimulated now by the sounds of the sea, memories of my short-lived battles with the icy wastes of the North Atlantic were flickering by like an old video. Staggering to the ship's galley from the foredeck, I was trying to make tea in between trips to the rails on the leeward side. The galley boy, all of nine months older, surveyed with lofty amusement my rubber-legged attempts to stay upright.

'Seen yeh ring yet?' he asked after my fifth trip to the rails. The joke was definitely wearing thin.

After he stopped laughing, he explained. 'Oh,' was all I could manage as a retort.

'Why'd you come to sea?' he asked, the ice now broken. 'I mean, you're pretty bloody useless on deck.'

I ignored this pleasantry as the ship gave a particularly vicious lurch. 'I wanted to get a pair of jeans,' I said. 'Levis, like yours.' I knew another fifteen-year-old would understand. Outside, there was a distant approaching roar of water as the ship heeled over.

'These?' he said. 'I got these in Leeds last week. Imports . . .'

The rest was drowned by a huge wall of water which smashed into the side of the ship, removed the lifeboat, shot into the galley, and bounced me off the bulkhead. The galley boy, of course, like everybody else, remained welded to the spot. As I was poured from one side of the galley to the other with the rest of the debris, the bosun appeared at the door.

'Never mind learning t'swim,' he said. 'Where's that bloody tea?'

Looking at the gentle waves breaking almost apologetically against the Suffolk beach on this perfect summer evening, it all seemed a long, long time ago and, unlike Southwold, I had no desire to live in the past. I pinched Pugwash to see if I was still awake.

'Yep,' I said, as Pugs bit me absentmindedly, one eye still warily on the sea.

'This is the seaside and we are at it, kid.' Pugs was unimpressed.

I jumped up. 'Last one in for a paddle's a sissy!' I yelled, running towards the ale-dark sea. It was no contest.

'This is the seaside and we are at it, kid.' Pugs was unimpressed.

10
Cat in a Basket

On that section of the east coast between Spurn Point and Flamborough Head centred on Aldbrough, chicken in a basket reigns supreme. Further south, on the Suffolk Heritage coast centred on Aldeburgh, the clear favourite is a certain cat in a basket. Exactly what this says about the North-South divide remains a bit of a mystery, but one fact is indisputable. A cat on a beach, in or out of a basket, is a guaranteed crowd-puller on the Suffolk coast.

This had put a certain strain upon the ongoing travelling relationship between me and said cat. In ad-speak, Pugs might be described as user friendly, slightly past his sell-by date, and with bad snack habits . . . which just about sums me up too, now I come to think about it. Whatever: when I arrived back from a snacking binge at some local café, I was likely to find an inevitable little crowd of old ladies gathered around The Beach Basket Cat. Where they came from or how the word spread was as mysterious as the Arctic tern navigating south for the winter. One minute the beach was empty; the next we would be surrounded by an adoring circle of Pugwash Groupies asking the same old questions.

'Is he yours?'

'(Sigh) Yes.'

Pugwash eyes me ironically. In terms of who owns whom, he may have a point.

'Does he like the beach?'

'Oh yes.'

Pugwash tries to bite me.

'Who's an icky little pussy den?' (Heave!)

Pugwash does a quick preen.

'Does he need much looking after?'

65

The Beach Basket Cat: a guaranteed crowd-puller on the Suffolk coast.

Pugs and I exchange glances. My answer will clearly provide a basis for future negotiations. I decide to err on the side of generosity. 'Nooo. Much easier than a dog.'

This proves to be a mistake. Given minimal encouragement, Pugwash immediately launches into his virtuoso performance of A Cat On A Hot Summer Beach for the adoring circle of fans.

We have the cat washing his face with one paw, and then the other (Ahhh). Then the hind leg stuck in the air routine as he grooms his tail (Ooohh). This is followed by the full stretch and yawn (Gosh), and for the Grande Finale—Pugwash lying on his back and kicking all four legs in the air at the same time.

'When a cat rolls over onto its back and lets you stroke its front, it's actually a sign of an animal giving you its complete and total trust,' says an ancient and very naïve fan.

'When this cat rolls over on his back,' I whisper through gritted teeth to the extravagantly prone Pugwash, 'it's actually the sign of an animal making a complete and total prat of himself while trying to cop an extra feed. So knock it off, gannet.'

Pugwash trudges back to his basket for a sulk, and the crowd disperses, twittering fond farewells to the cat basket as they go, and leaving me in peace until the next performance. At last I was left alone to consider this part of the Suffolk coast between Dunwich and Aldeburgh.

Dunwich is a strange place, particularly on a stormy, dark night. Once a thriving town, only one street of houses remains, and even in high summer the village seems bleakly haunted by its past, most of which is somewhere off the steeply raked beach, thanks to the coastal erosion. Parked overnight (illegally) in the beach car park, and with the wind blowing mournfully off the marsh that stretches north to Walberswick, it required little imagination to summon up the ghostly community of Dunwich past.

Even Pugs, who was prone to wander after sunset, stayed close to the van and I carefully locked all the doors. When a large furry face made a sudden, unscheduled appearance outside the windscreen, I leaped up, knocked the gas lamp over, and banged about in the dark for several minutes, cursing cats in general and one in particular. Only later did it occur to me that someone was exacting sweet revenge. And I tried not to feel too guilty as I drifted off under the duvet, lulled to sleep by the occasional heartrending cries from one outraged cat left out all night to brave the monsoon rains of an English summer. Life on the road can get very petty sometimes.

The next morning revealed a seascape as delicate as a Japanese print. The Suffolk Heritage coast would not please lovers of excess. Its strengths lie in the chiaroscuro effects of sea and sky, and subtle colour gradations of the marsh reedbeds and the fragile fretwork of trees on the inland skyline. And over it all, a product of the flat land next to the sea, looms the huge sky, providing a spectacular amphitheatre for the weather. No wonder the prevailing mood here was one of nostalgia, that peculiarly English sad sense of loss for a past that may or may not have existed.

All of this made Sizewell A, a huge, windowless concrete obscenity that dominates the coastline from Southwold to Aldeburgh, harder to take. And now Sizewell B was well under way; the 40 metres deep diaphragm wall—optimistically being built to prevent a future China Syndrome—churned up that once beautiful coastal walk from Minsmere to Sizewell, adding insult to injury.

More disturbing, however, was the man I met in the Leiston pub, just two miles from the site. Newly hired and exuberant after 14 months on the dole, he was planning to bring his wife and young family down from Sheffield in a few weeks' time. He spent all his spare time cycling around the small roads and lanes around Leiston, like someone newly released from confinement, which in a way he had been.

A seascape as delicate as a Japanese print.

Sizewell B was well under way.

Only later and after several pints did the cracks start to show. It wasn't true, was it, about the cancer scares? They'd told him there was no real evidence. He changed the subject but kept coming back to it, unable to leave it alone. Did I think it was true? I said I wasn't sure either, but yes, I thought it was possible there was a link.

'That more bairns get cancer in these places?' he repeated.

What the hell do you say to someone in this predicament, putting not just himself—'I don't mind me,' he'd said several times— but his family at possible risk for the sake of a job? And then the subject changed again as he circled like a moth around some unthinkable

69

flame. He was going to get a second bike and fit them both with carry-frames so that he and his wife could take the two bairns and explore the countryside. 'They've never seen countryside like this,' he said, 'or the beaches. We'll explore all over.'

And I sat there thinking that, wherever he went, those grotesque, eyeless buildings would follow him like an incurable infection. Each everyday cough and sniffle of the children, every schoolyard bruise, ache, or pain, would be magnified and distorted into possibly something else that didn't bear thinking about. And I doubted if the CEGB had included any of that on his job description.

Moving on through the Edwardian theme park of Thorpeness—theme 'Loads A Money'—I finally arrived at Aldeburgh with one beach-struck cat. Here the favoured uniform of the locals was jeans and big fishermen's sweaters, and once again I was reminded that the peculiar English demarcation of dressing down or dressing up when relaxing depended upon which side of the tracks you came from. Aldeburgh was a pleasant enough place; but another Aldbrough, like another country, was beckoning. It was time to leave the fat south lands and head for the lean north. I looked at Pugwash, sitting in his basket on the passenger seat and looking profoundly bored without an audience.

'Up there,' I said, 'they do things differently.' Pugwash yawned.

'For starters, they eat chicken in a basket. So don't get clever. Mistakes have been known to occur. Right?'

It was probably a trick of the light as he gave himself a quick wash. But I could have sworn he stuck his tongue out.

11
Old Broads and the Costa Brid

Arriving on the coast of East Yorkshire without a cat made me feel rather like Hannibal without his elephants. Pugwash was acclimatising with a cat-loving aunt while I explored the highs and lows of northern seaside life. I was not, however, alone. A friend, John Hewitt, was standing in for the furry one. And at six foot seven with a shock of bright red hair, he attracted almost as much attention. There was something vaguely Laurel and Hardy about us as we navigated our way round, with that same sense of high farce skating perilously close to impending disaster.

Aldbrough was a case in point. This part of Holderness has supposedly the most rapid coastal erosion in the country: witness the road to the beach that stops abruptly in mid-air. My maternal grandfather bought a bungalow there in the 'fifties and I have vague memories of sunburn and nettle rash. Not a lucky man, he chose a cliff-top bungalow for the view and the sunrise. Which was why, at low tide now, we could just about see where it had been.

There were two pubs in the village and the second one contained Ray. Valiantly flying the flag as Aldbrough's Hell's Angel, his large tattooed frame zoomed around the bar in a wheelchair—the legacy of a motorcycle accident—that frequently threatened lift-off. One of nature's survivors, the fact that only one limb out of four worked properly seemed about as disabling as a sprained ankle and nothing short of World War Three would curb his natural exuberance.

After closing time we drove to the cliff top and parked for the night by an abandoned amusement arcade that would soon be feeding the voracious North Sea. Talking quietly against a background of wind and surf—I was still adjusting to the novelty of a travelling companion who talked back—we didn't notice the car

71

At Aldbrough the road to the beach stops abruptly in mid-air.

without lights until it stopped nearby and the interior light came on, revealing two men.

John went rigid. 'They've got a shot gun,' he whispered. And so they had.

'They might use us as a target,' breathed John, switching off our interior light.

'They might be homophobics and think we're gay,' I hyperventilated, switching the light back on.

The light went off and on like a lighthouse as the argument raged back and forth. Meanwhile the two farmers in the car drove off after presumably completing the inspection and sale of the shot gun—the probable explanation that occurred in the cold light of next day's dawn. Later, listening to the surf crashing into the base of the crumbling cliff as we turned in, another thought occurred.

'Erm. You don't think we're too near the edge, do you?' said a muffled voice from the depths of a sleeping bag.

'Solid as a rock,' I said, winding down the window to provide a possible quick escape. Given two hyperactive imaginations in a confined space, it was going to be a long night.

The next day we arrived at Bridlington, renowned for its fine EEC-approved beaches and colourful after-hours street fighting. Staggering from a gigantic breakfast at Alf's Nosh Bar, we launched ourselves in separate directions to sample the traditional bums and knickers atmosphere of Brid. I used to love the place as a kid and still have a soft spot for it. It has a raunchy style and large numbers of pensioners add an appropriate anarchic touch. If the late-night streets belong to gangs of youths hell-bent on a bed-time knuckle sandwich, the days belong to OAPs hell-bent on reliving their own days of wine and roses.

And there is an endearing casual matiness that even extends to the public toilets (now, now) where each cubicle has a little glass window. I looked from the morning newspaper to see the smiling face of the attendant beaming down through mine.

' 'Aving a good clear-out?' he asked conversationally.

'Yes, thank you.'

'That's the way,' he said, ambling off and whistling 'No Regrets'.

Joining the wandering crowd of holidaymakers endlessly window shopping, I kept seeing the same faces including, eventually, John's. We headed for the Cock and Lion by the harbour to watch the seemingly immortal Tassie Hamilton accompanied by the Mike Edwards Sound. Entering, we got blitzed by a 'Strangers in the Night' medley played by the man himself in a Costa Brid hat and a perilously stretched T-shirt. The music—played on a relentlessly jolly organ—was of the follow-the-bouncing-ball school, and heads nodded in unison as the music staggered seamlessly into the holiday anthem, 'Viva Espana'.

Finally the star of the show was announced. 'A Mega-Star in her own mind! Famous all over the world in Brid! Fresh from entertaining the troops at the Battle of the Somme! 78 years young! (True.) Tassie Hamilton!'

And on to the cleared floor space leaped an extraordinary figure wearing black riding boots, fish-net tights, a slashed red mini skirt, and big red knickers.

'Come t'see the old cow perform?' she leers. 'Or whether she's snuffed it!'

As Tassie roars into her act, several people in wheelchairs are rolled in looking—perhaps understandably—apprehensive. They needn't. 'Where you from, love?' yells Tassie to one of them. 'Wales? Where they get outa the bath to 'ave a pee!'

'I took a girl to Wales once,' chimes in Mike. 'To Bangor.'

Leeds, Bradford, Doncaster, Hull: they all come in for the same quick-fire treatment as the unstoppable Tassie grabs the audience by the throat—and other parts. She plonks herself on a delighted old man's knee.

'Moved to tears, love?' she simpers, as his wife glares daggers. 'Nah . . . his eyes are watering. I've just squashed 'is knackers!'

She hoists a leg over his shoulder.

'Funny place t'keep a hedgehog,' wonders somebody aloud, and the act roars on. And so do John and I.

The jokes against Poofs, Lezzies, and Pakis would rightly have caused the wrong kind of riot on the Alternative Cabaret circuit: but in her own inimitable way Tassie also confounded deeply entrenched prejudices about old people. The old are not even supposed to think about sex, let alone do it. And, unlike the young, who desperately conform to their own standards, old people—given half a chance—are naturally anarchic.

Witness the scene over at the Harbour Lites where Duette—'Direct from a winter season in Los Americas' (Where?) led an entire

(Opposite) *The days belong to OAPs hell-bent on reliving their days of wine and roses.*
Tassie Hamilton, Mega-Star of the Costa Brid.

TASSIE HAMILTON'S
KNEES UP
with the
ZANY
MIKE
DWARDS
SOUND

Lunch served 1

nto. Bar till 2am.

roomful of pensioners in a raucous sing-song. Old Harry, who could barely walk and who 'comes from Hull twice a week special', was half-carried onto the stage and sat on a chair. The fact that he was facing the wrong way—off stage—and could only move his head, became an irrelevance as he belted out a medley of Al Jolson numbers. He was a sensation and the audience of over-65s were away, singing, swaying, and yelling for favourites.

As the afternoon pounded on, couples became more and more affectionate, and over at the singles bar the comments moved from the suggestive—'she could owld two weeks' rain in them wrinkles—round 'er arse: and I could drink every drop'—to the unprintable. Finally Harry was carried off the stage on a great wave of cheers and applause; and John and I staggered out into the mid-afternoon rain feeling very, very old. Brid was a great place to visit, but I didn't think I could live there. I could never stand the pace.

12
The Cat o' Nine Naughty Tales

'How could you?' I said to the back of Pugwash's head for the tenth time. We were driving across the North Yorkshire moors and the late summer rain was sheeting almost horizontally across the narrow road ahead. Pugwash examined the back of his basket with an intense concentration usually reserved for food. The ears lying close to the head, however, told a different story. This was a cat in deep trouble, and he knew it.

'She loved that budgie,' I said. 'She thought the sun shone out of its beak. It could speak,' I said pointedly. 'Several words.' Two ears were lowered by another millimetre.

As I have already mentioned, Pugwash had been parked briefly with an (ex) cat-loving aunt of mine near Hull. Two years before, she had replaced her beloved stiffed Tiddles—a ludicrous name for a vastly overweight cat that spread out like a small rug when it lay on the floor—with a budgie called George.

'Nothing will ever replace Tiddles,' she'd said. But George had. The fact that George occasionally laid eggs never deterred her, although it does go some way to explain why she's my only maiden aunt. Conditioned presumably by a long association with the Cyril Smith of the cat world, she made a disastrous miscalculation with a deceptively laid-back Pugs. After several months on the road, we were dealing here with a serious hunter.

'I'd just let George out for his little flutter,' said my still bemused aunt, 'when bang! All I could see was a little cloud of feathers and your cat with a funny look on its face.'

And all I could see was a cat apparently without ears studiously doing his homework on basketwork. The wind slashed the rain across the windscreen.

This was a cat in deep trouble, and he knew it.

'Well, bang,' I said, 'go my chances for that cuckoo clock I'd had my eye on. Funny look, hey? You—comedian!'

*   *   *

It had not been the best of weekends. After transporting an emotional and overtired artist from wildest Bridlington to the relative if occasionally homicidal refuge of south London, I had spent a couple of days in Brockley. I was looking forward to a rare and peaceful Pugwash-free domestic weekend. Yes . . .

Glancing out of the kitchen window on the Saturday afternoon, I noticed two squirrels apparently bonking at the bottom of the garden. On closer inspection, one seemed to be trying to eat the other. Given what goes on sometimes in parked cars near the bottom of that garden, it was not a particular cause for concern. And then I saw the blood. By the time I reached the scene, the grey hooligan was half-way up the nearest tree, leaving his victim in a sorry state: unconscious, blood-stained, and racked by convulsions. I briefly considered putting it out of its misery, but then copped out. The RSPCA would know what to do.

'Are you sure it's an emergency?' asked the emergency service.

'Oh yes, it's on its last legs. Blood everywhere. Pain . . .'

'We'll be there in half an hour,' said the capable voice, reassuringly.

I'd placed the squirrel in a plastic bowl and put it in an empty room upstairs. Its mentor arrived in the shape of a huge man with the biggest hands I've ever seen. We trooped upstairs and I opened the door quietly. The animal was now sitting upright but with its head drooping to the floor. There was no movement.

'I think it's gone,' I whispered, and right on cue it opened one baleful eye and then the other.

'I don't think so,' said the large-handed man authoritatively. The squirrel glared up at us fixedly. With the benefit of hindsight, I wonder why I automatically assume losers are always nice.

'Perhaps it's going into a coma,' I said gently.

'I don't think so,' said the ham-fisted one cautiously.

I moved towards it. 'I wouldn't do that, actually,' he said.

'Why?'

These were the last calm words that anyone uttered for some time. The squirrel suddenly appeared to levitate as it powered towards us.

'Look out!' we both yelled as we dived in different directions.

The miraculously arisen squirrel bounced off the door between us, spun round, and crouched for another pounce. A thought crossed my mind. 'You don't think it could have—rabies, do you?'

'It's a possibility.'

And the squirrel was between us and door.

Suddenly it pounced again, and there was another bout of yells and scuffles. There then followed a ludicrous sequence as two grown men ran around a room pursued by a kamikaze squirrel.

'This is ridiculous,' I gasped.

'Tell him that,' panted the RSPCA man.

Suddenly the squirrel ran out of steam, and so did I. Professional training and big hands came to the fore. Scooping the squirrel up by its tail, he ran down the stairs and through the garden and dropped it over a cemetery wall. When last seen, it was attacking a stone angel.

'I'm sorry,' I said as he was leaving. 'I really thought . . .'

'Don't worry,' he said reassuringly. 'It takes all sorts.'

Only later did it occur he was referring to me.

So much for a quiet weekend in Brockley. Meanwhile, back on the Yorkshire Moors with the Wrath of Budgies, the weather was starting to improve. The night before I'd parked by the lighthouse at Flamborough Head. A full gale was forecast and by midnight the spokes of light were revolving through a howling wind and great sheets of spindrift from the waves were crashing against the cliffs below. By morning the van was covered in salt and, due to an oversight (hand on heart), so was a certain cat. I'd assumed he was asleep on the front seat when I closed the windows against the gale. The next morning I opened them to admit an enraged, salt-encrusted Pugwash.

'Call it divine retribution, kid,' I said, avoiding the claws as I brushed the worst of the salt out. Cats rarely see the funny side of acts of God.

By the time I arrived at Robin Hood's Bay, the rain had died away, the sun was out, and Pugwash was comatose, dreaming presumably of giant, salt-encrusted budgies. I parked at the top of the one-in-three that tumbles the houses down to the narrow entrance to the huge bay, and walked down. The last time I had come here it was in the dead of winter. The surrounding moors were deep in snow and the place was all but cut off. Then, all the talk in the village was about the headless corpse of a woman that had just been found on the beach after a storm. One of the suicides, probably, who

(Opposite) By morning the van was covered in salt and, due to an oversight (hand on heart), so was a certain cat.

sometimes come to the great cliffs below Ravenscar on the last stage of some private hellish journey. There was also a sense of isolation and insularity, with the bitter east wind battering against the closed and shuttered houses, and the quiet gossip in the pub perhaps even more ferocious than the wind.

Like all seaside places, the village has two lives and the winter life may well be the more truthful. Now, walking through the small crowd of holidaymakers determined to snatch a few memories from the last days of a catastrophic summer, the place had a familiar gloss on it. Selfconsciously upmarket from Brid and Filey, it attracts a fair number of green wellies and—given the close proximity of the moors—bobble hats and walking boots. But Ye Olde Crafte Shoppe and Local Artists exhibition manage to contain the same dire results that escapees from the rat race inflict on pliant tourists the country over. I sometimes imagine they all attend the same evening class in arts and crafts somewhere near Hebden Bridge and emerge with a Local Artists Diploma in Dodgy Printmaking and Ethnic Mugs.

At the landing by the Bay Hotel, the tiny King's Beck, architect of the little valley, swept under the base of scaffolding creeping up the face of the hotel. The scaffolders, heroes of the building trade, paraded their fine physiques before a relaxed throng of admiring women and irritated husbands and boyfriends. I leaned over the parapet at the hotel to watch their casual skill fifty feet above the beach. Overhead the inevitable seagulls whirled. 'I should watch it,' said one amiably. 'Them shite hawks can crap through the eye of a needle.'

'And what would you do if a bird crapped on your head?' another asked him.

'I dunno,' he said, 'but I don't think I'd go out with 'er agen.'

Sitting on the parapet, warmed by the cheerful banter, the fitful sunshine and a third pint, I started to generate a few good memories of my own. Across the bay the low tide had revealed the rock strata

(Opposite) *I parked at the top of the one-in-three that tumbles the houses down to the huge bay.*

strewn with glistening strands of seaweed. Over them Lowry's matchstick figures wandered, looking for fossils and effortlessly making the point that artistic talent really can make you see the world through their eyes.

That evening I sat high on the moors with a salt-free and, judging by the ears, guilt-free cat. I'd taken some trouble to find this exalted and isolated spot, well away from the small side road. On the drive up, the valley below had slowly revealed itself like a summer picnic. Now it was a great dark bowl sprinkled with the lights of distant hill farms. Maybe it was the chill wind or the purple haze of the surrounding heather. More likely it was Pugwash resuming his early habit of warming his great feet on me at night. Whatever, it felt like summer was over. And so was my visit to Yorkshire, apparently.

As Pugs and I watched the midnight movie—*Curse of the Mummy's Tomb*—with all the doors locked and windows firmly closed, a car suddenly appeared, lights glared and two faces under peaked caps peered in. I opened the window.

'Evening,' said one. 'Staying the night?'

'It crossed my mind,' I said, still under the duvet.

'Moving on tomorrow, then?' asked the other.

'Oh yes,' I said. Six months on I was definitely roadwise.

'See you do,' he said pleasantly.

We exchanged names and addresses—theirs was The Police from Yorkshire, by the way—and they drove off.

'Well,' I said, as someone was decapitated on the small screen, 'that's the first time we've been thrown out of Yorkshire.' Pugwash concentrated on warming his feet. 'It was probably all your fault anyway,' I said, snuggling under the duvet to watch the Mummy pursue a beautiful and very bad actress. 'They've probably got you and that budgie on the computer.' Pugwash feigned sleep.

(Opposite) I sat high on the moors with a salt-free and, judging by the ears, guilt-free cat.

13
Claws II

They were burning the fields as we drove west, me and the incorrigible one. At a distance the sound was ironically like running water. The nose of Pugwash was glued to the windscreen: anything to alleviate the boredom of a long-distance drive. Having left the east coast rather suddenly, we were heading for Wales.

Suddenly a great hare, miraculously unscathed, appeared by the charcoaled field and leaped across the road ahead. I slammed on the brakes and, with the marvellous reflexes of his breed, Pugs hopped sideways onto my lap and dug four sets of claws in for anchorage. Battling with a long, slow skid—not to mention a perforated crutch—I slid gently round a bend in the road, and there revealed below was the little town of Kington set against a background of the Welsh Borders. I was immediately ambushed by *déjà vu*.

Back in the early 'seventies, when all the world was new, I'd bought a share in a communally owned property—The Talbot—in this small country border town. The fact that there were thirteen of us was an omen we all chose to ignore at the time. As I shuddered to a stop and extracted a rigid cat from an even more rigid groin, memories revived of the great dialectical battles of the past. The theory of labour's surplus value and its relevance to taking the rubbish out. Washing up: was it an intrinsically sexist occupation, or only when the women partners did it? Was all property theft? If so, were we all thieves? and did Genet's views on crime alleviate our position? Who'd liberated Simon's half grapefruit from the 'fridge and exactly how did this action equate with the rape of Third World countries by the multinationals? (We discovered it didn't, actually.)

Stalled at the top of the hill with a throbbing groin and a cat in the middle of a panic wash, I watched the little town below emerge into the twilight of the evening like a slowly developing photograph. Unreliable memories were tending to push the good times to the front of the crowd like proud but anxious parents. Common sense reminded me there were bad times, too.

Across the valley was Bradnor Hill, once the home of the reclusive Mike Oldfield. On the opposite side was Hergest Ridge, subject of his second opus. Given the long journey, I decided to spend the night upon Hergest and leave memory lane for another day. I fell asleep wondering if they made seat belts for cats.

During the night a storm blew up, and by morning wild, blustery weather was sweeping the twelve hundred foot ridge. Cunningly concealed in a wood, I was feeling pleased with myself. So was Pugwash, who had clearly worked off his anxiety attack on the local small mammal population.

Cunningly concealed in a wood, I was feeling pleased with myself. So was Pugwash.

'Listen, Attila,' I said, as I removed the neat little row of corpses, 'if this goes on, you'll be the only moggy in Herefordshire wearing a muzzle.' Undeterred, Pugwash slept the dreamless sleep of an entirely fulfilled cat.

Down in the town, the half-empty, rain-swept High Street belied the date. The second Saturday in September is always the day of the Kington Show. And not once had I ever been. Ignoring the dog show—I didn't want any arguments from old radar nose later—I wandered onto the sodden recreation ground, and found myself in another world.

Kington now has a lively mix of a community which sometimes belies the fact that agriculture was and still is the staple industry in the area. Five minutes into the show would confirm that: as would the huge list of the general committee, stewards, and exhibitors in the official programme. It was not difficult to see why so many of that first wave of refugees from the cities foundered on these vast, intractable columns.

What I was looking at was a trade fair, annual Celtic blood-letting, and gathering of the clans, all rolled into one. More than that, though, I was suddenly in the middle of a thriving but largely invisible community that kept to itself in the surrounding hills and countryside and emerged collectively for this one day of the year. And such communities are not built to be gate-crashed.

Recently concern was expressed for the Good and Not So Good Lifers who flee the inverted values of the cities—particularly London, where all needs are increasingly objectified (you are what you drive, babe)—and find themselves trapped in the sometimes suicidal isolation of the hills. Of the 4,000 callers to the Samaritans in nearby Aberystwyth and mid-Wales in 1986, two-thirds were migrants to the area and a chilling quarter of them were suicidal. Like the past, this area can be the most foreign of countries: and they certainly like to do things differently.

As the day wore on, the rain eased and finally stopped and the crowd swelled to cheer on the trotting racers or examine with a critical and practised eye cattle and sheep that were so immaculate, they appeared to have been shampooed, set, and blow-dried. And maybe they had. I was confronted by the apparently permed bum of a massive, prize-winning bull. As I stood transfixed by his giant appendages hanging halfway to the ground, a genial farmer, who had clearly overdone the ale tent, put a friendly arm around my shoulder.

''Tween ourselves,' he breathed beerily, ''e 'as trouble getting it up.' I was not surprised. It would probably take a fork-lift truck and several strong men. For the first time in my life, I felt sorry for cows.

Nearby, a pair of ewes looked so pretty it suddenly became very easy to believe all those rumours about shepherds and wellington boots. Elsewhere horse people, dressed to perfection from fetlock to forelock, posed by horses so patiently still they appeared from the side to be one-dimensional cardboard cut-outs. The Shire horses, on the other hand, were so loaded with horse brass they looked like four-legged versions of Mr T.

In and around all this, of course, was a quietly ferocious undercurrent of competition. Feuds that began here could span generations. The tightly buttoned Welsh Chapel conformism is a bizarre straitjacket for a Celtic temperament and probably goes some way to explaining this strange manic-depressive race. So I stand in awe at the courage of those judges who volunteer to put themselves in the firing line of all that misplaced passion—seen at its peak in the Domestic tent. Here, leeks the size of small goal posts stood proudly next to football-sized onions. Close by the winning entries, stone-faced losers stood muttering. And whoever judged the cakes deserved a medal. It must take nerves of steel to place somebody third and go on living in the same small town with them.

Over these dangerous cross-currents drifted bizarre announcements as the Flying Gunners motorcycle team went through their paces. 'And neoww!' echoed the Tannoy. 'The Single Beezer!'

The immaculately dressed farmer next to me was unmoved, his mind on higher things. ''E were determined to give 'im furst. Determined,' he said to his son, who wore a 'Who Bares Wins' T-shirt and leaned perilously to the right.

I found Pugwash enthusiastically sharpening his claws in anticipation of that night's carnage.

'The Double Beezer!'

'Never 'ardly looked at mine. Walked straight parst,' he rumbled on as men and machines flew through the air with reckless abandon.

'The Tulip!'

'I . . . reckon' mumbled his son, and trailed off as he lost the unequal struggle with gravity.

'Reckon you've 'ad enough, man,' said the farmer to his now horizontal son, and continued: 'Straight parst.'

(Opposite) Sheep that were so immaculate, they appeared to have been shampooed, set and blow-dried. And maybe they had.

'The Kaleidoscope!' echoed the Tannoy as I was leaving the recreation ground. I passed a line of beautifully renovated old farm oil engines, still working magically and surrounded by a throng of excited, chattering, boyish men.

That evening, I walked across the top of Hergest Ridge. The wind had dropped and the sunset took its natural course under a magnificent sky you only ever seem to get in the west. Hergest is shaped like a great whale and straddles the border. Look east and you see the cluttered populous patchwork quilt of Herefordshire and England. Look west and the rounded Black Mountains of Powys stretch away to the horizon.

I have never understood why to travel west is somehow to move away from the past towards (perhaps) a new start and a different future. But generations of European migrants have thought so. And I felt the same magnetic pull myself once and feel it faintly still. And others continue to come and some will manage to stay, while others, like tourists, will bring their own cultural baggage and defend themselves with inappropriate values and fail and leave.

Arriving back at the van I discovered Pugwash enthusiastically sharpening his claws in anticipation of that night's carnage. Cats, of course, have an entirely appropriate set of values for all occasions and are notoriously adaptable. They are all blessed with short-term memories and are rarely troubled by the past.

'Of course,' I said to a particularly vacant-looking Pugwash, 'some are shorter than others.' Perhaps he was labouring to remember who he was and why he was here. But when I followed the line of his fixed gaze, I saw he was eyeing a wood pigeon in a nearby tree. Existentialism never was his strong point.

14
The Vengeance of Vindaloo

The colourful wash of autumn was finally sweeping through the woods and hedgerows on the Welsh borders. Back in Brockley the trees, victims of London's micro-climate, should be well on the turn; as would the local gang of feline reprobates. Cats are not terribly impressed by the season of mists and mellow fruitfulness. Basically, it gets colder. Which is why I usually end up at this time of year with a row of anxious, bewhiskered faces peering in through the window. As a matter of fact, I could see one outside the van at that moment with not unfamiliar markings, peering down from a nearby tree. And thereby hung a tale.

Of late, Uno Macho had rather had it all his own way. Mainly because he was usually the biggest animal around, he had developed a tendency to swagger about his woody domain. In another reincarnation, he would probably have been wearing his shirt open to the waist and flashing a large gold St Christopher. His nemesis arrived one morning in the guise of three sheepdogs from a nearby farm on the flanks of Hergest Ridge.

Now I should really make the distinction here between pet dogs and working dogs. Particularly the variety that work on Welsh hill farms. As Pugwash found to his cost, it's sometimes difficult to believe they belong to the same species. Huge, shaggy and blank eyed with contained violence, they spend their lives outdoors hunting, in theory if not in practice, large herds of sheep.

There is no such animal as a fat, breathless, pampered Welsh sheepdog. Not a lot of cats from Brockley know this. Which is why, when the trio spotted Pugs from a nearby field and homed in, he took his time ambling into the wood. Seconds before three sets of snarling jaws propelled him into that great cat litter tray in the sky, and certainly too late for me to intervene, it obviously dawned on him that standing sideways on his tiptoes and making his tail fat to look bigger was not fooling anybody. Throwing caution—and dignity—to the winds, he shot up a handy tree inches ahead of several dozen teeth.

Which was why a small wood on a Welsh hillside now contained the only known species of domestic cat that spends its entire outdoor life up a tree. When I felt like cheering myself up, I would open the van window, wave, and give a Tarzan-like yodel. Pugs would pretend not to notice. Cats hate to make prats of themselves. But then, don't we all?

There was, however, another reason for frequently opening the windows. The previous night we had indulged in an Indian takeaway, old Iron Gut and I. This led to an interesting discovery. Mutton Vindaloo from the Welsh Borders and the confined space of a Ford Transit are not compatible. Around midnight a sound like a distant herd of trumpeting elephants rose and fell. The Vengeance of Vindaloo was at hand. This was immediately followed by another sound, like a wasp in a bottle. Pugwash, who had snaffled most of the Mutton Tikka, never could resist a challenge.

I had spent much of the necessarily sleepless night ruminating over my brief communal days in this area during the 'seventies. Misreading the fundamentals of a species is not always the prerogative of tree-bound cats. Take the Open Relationship era, for instance.

Those readers with flares marinating among the moth balls may remember that particular hiccup in the long march of monogamy. It usually began with a late night theoretical discussion—always a bad sign, this—on the true nature of relationships, their essential dynamics and, in particular, how having other relationships could enrich the current one without posing a threat. That's right. The eating-your-mate-and-having-it school of thought. The opening gambit was rather like the proverbial tip of the iceberg.

(Opposite) The only known species of domestic cat that spends its entire outdoor life up a tree.

'Would you mind?'

'Erm, no . . . Would you?'

'Oh, no . . . Really.'

Ten little words that opened up the Pandora's Box of the 'seventies. Two friends of mine actually went on Radio 4 at the time to extol the virtues of the Open Relationship. A few weeks later, she discovered he'd been enthusiastically putting theory into practice for over two years. Running upstairs, she hurled all the bedroom furniture through the window and immediately felt better than she had done for months.

Only politicians, social scientists, dingbats and the Pope presume to fathom the mysteries of the human heart. Personally, I found it absolutely no problem in my Kington days when I enriched a relationship. The trouble started when t'other one started mulching. Oddly enough, she felt exactly the same way. It's a funny old world.

Back in the van, the elephants were getting closer. Audibly annoyed and looking for trouble, they succeeded in irritating the wasp in the bottle. It was beginning to sound like the soundtrack of *Out of Africa.* Any moment now Karen Blixen would turn up with an Oscar, Robert Redford and syphilis, although not necessarily in that order.

Drifting off again, I found myself on a long, slow slide into that most English of vices. Nostalgia, actually. Nostalgia is a two-faced thing, forever looking backwards and re-ordering the past in preparation for the next step forward. Insidious, though, because sometimes the past becomes so appealing when set against an increasingly difficult present that the next step never materialises. And then, like something preserved in amber, people get stuck in some improbable past.

There are, of course, people like that around the Welsh Borders, although far fewer than you might imagine. Gentle, confused, almost middle-aged people who enthuse about the recent progress in arms talks on the grounds that a third world war might delay Cat Stevens' comeback.

Meanwhile, back on the savannah, the elephants had produced a final defiant cacophony before dwindling into the distance. The wasp in the bottle had retaliated by metamorphosing into an entire hornets' nest, and Pugwash appeared to levitate several inches before slowly descending. Which was another reason why Britain's only tree cat was gazing into the van rather wistfully this evening from the safety of his nearby perch.

Earlier in the day, as it was market day in Kington, I watched as the livestock were shunted and poked and jammed into pens for auction and slaughter. The terrified animals, with holes punched through their ears, and spattered with blood, stood in their own waste and mess and misery, and I had difficulty remaining neutral.

Perhaps this showed more than I imagined. After a few minutes a rather nervous auctioneer appeared and asked me to move on. In the nearest pub, men stained with shit and blood stood with legs apart like aggressive letter As, hands in pockets, talking loudly about the previous night's triumphs, and who had done what to which woman. Even the would-be jokes all seemed to be about blood and shit. Maybe handling animals at this stage—as in the abattoirs— brutalises people. Or perhaps the work just attracts them.

I watched as the livestock were shunted and poked and jammed into pens.

Later, after the stockmen had left, poor mad Hilda entered. I remembered her from my days at The Talbot and I almost believed, fleetingly, that she remembered me as she hesitated and then passed on to her corner. There she nodded and smiled and chattered to herself and endlessly broke bread into small pieces, as she had done for years.

Her companion, perhaps her husband, whistled non-stop and stared off into the distance. But he always treated her with gentle concern, as did the landlord and all the regulars. I wondered what her chances would be in London. As the government enthusiastically throws the mentally fragile onto the tender mercies of community care, perhaps it has in mind this scene in Kington. The only problem is that, for community care, you first need a community.

As the evening light faded and the mists moved in among the trees to shroud the details of the wood, one particular cat-shaped detail continued to stand out. Autumn always was my favourite season, and the melancholy softness of the light and the colours never fail to reach me. I looked up at the stubborn outline and, like the season itself, felt myself mellowing. I opened the window again and gave a sympathetic yodel. As the last of the birdsong died with the light, a distant sound drifted down from the tree like a wraith of mist. It sounded remarkably like a wasp trapped in a bottle.

As the evening light faded, one particular cat-shaped detail continued to stand out.

15
Magic Mushrooms—and Homicidal Mammary Glands

Two days later I found myself parked on Hays Bluff, well over a thousand feet above the Wye Valley. I had been privileged to observe, at first hand and very close quarters, the remarkable rituals of certain species when preparing for the onset of long nights and dark winter. Well, one of a species, anyway. A certain cat, actually.

The day before, for example, we had been blasted by storm-force winds that would have flattened most trees—if any could actually grow in this exposed and often desolate place. Therefore you might assume that your Moggy Domesticus would be inclined to get its head down until it all blew over. Certainly in Brockley they miraculously disappear into the woodwork or appear to be nailed to the floor in front of the fire when it comes to chucking-out time on dark and stormy autumn days. On Hays Bluff, however, things were a little different.

As I toiled away on the final part of a new play, I was frequently interrupted by the Incredible Flying Cat. As the wind roared across the blasted heath outside the van, Pugwash zoomed by, tail upright, eyes alight with mad joy like some demented Chinese kite. I could only assume that, in the wide open spaces, Pugs had finally made a discovery birds made long ago: that a strong following wind does wonders for lift-off. Well, hurray for Pugwash.

Unfortunately, defying gravity did not stop at whizzing downhill with a tail wind. An open window on each side of the van proved irresistible, and suddenly we had the Now-You-See-Me-Now-You-Don't Cat. Using the following winds, he sailed through one window, trampolined off the table and my notes—leaving four great

I was frequently interrupted by the Incredible Flying Cat.

muddy footmarks—and disappeared through the opposite open window with a joyful yell.

I intercepted the furry missile in mid-flight for a little heart to heart. Well, nose to nose anyway.

'Listen, Dick Head,' I hissed. 'Me—work. You—play. Right?'

It was like trying to persuade Joe Bugner he couldn't box.

After a few more vanishing cat routines, not to mention creeping hypothermia, I unthinkingly closed the offside window. A big mistake. Elevated by a particularly strong gust, our hero sailed through the open window and, with a single bound, catapulted into the closed window opposite. Undeterred, he did a mid-air somersault and landed on all muddy fours by the typewriter, scattering notes and coffee all over the table. Which was why at this very moment an unrepentant Chinese kite could be seen flying across the grass at some considerable distance from the van. Still, I suppose it's difficult to take life seriously when you run around all the time without any clothes on.

Pugwash was not the only one having a final fling before winter set in. Across the high fields, little groups of magic mushroom gatherers were scattered, looking like rather odd sheep as they grazed the area carefully with bulging plastic bags. Once several dozen New Age Travellers would gather up here for a final farewell (slightly) hallucinogenic binge. Today, I seemed to be the only one spending time here and the mushroom gatherers themselves were a motley crew. There were, of course, still some stereotypes from the old school: men with long pigtails and multiple earrings who seemed to come out of every sentence backwards. I asked two of them how you recognised a magic mushroom.

'It's like erm,' said one; trailing off glassy-eyed.

'Yeah,' said the other. 'Right.'

Eventually we got down to specifics.

'They're like tits, see,' one said, showing me his bagful.

'With nipples,' said the other carefully. And so they were. Very small ones.

'You need thirty for a good buzz.'

'Nah, fifty,' said the other.

'Fifty? Blow yeh frigging 'ead off, fifty.'

'Frigging won't.'

'Frigging will.'

I left them arguing over the correct number to sustain maximum brain damage, and remembered how magic mushrooms probably helped launched the Father Christmas legends. The Siberian nomads would eat them and then urinate a potent mixture onto the snow. Then the reindeer, presumably bored by the endless Siberian winter nights, would consume the spiked snow and join in the collective hallucinations around the communal hut. The nomads and reindeer probably encouraged each other to ever greater heights of disorientation with cries of the Siberian equivalent of 'Oh What!' and 'Too much, Man!'. And the most popular hallucination? Flying reindeer.

Down in Hay itself, a pleasant little border town where every other building, including the old fire station and cinema, seemed to be a bookshop—owned by the ubiquitous Richard Booth—the tourist

Hay-on-Wye: a pleasant little border town where every other building seemed to be a bookshop.

season was over. Hay-on-Wye has the same kind of reputation as Hebden Bridge: idiosyncratic, wacky, and a true heir to the mythical brown rice era. In both places this is simultaneously false and good for business. Personally I find something irritating about the frankly improbable image of the zany, lovable English eccentric.

A truly authentic individualist is Lucy Powell, who runs the Three Tuns, the 'Last Free House in Wales'. You might say in Britain. It is in fact one room, rather like a living-room, that has accumulated a lifetime's memorabilia. Faded pictures and objects clutter the walls and shelves and even the odd table and the small bar. The place is patrolled by three cats and an ancient smelly dog and Lucy holds court over it all like a friendly aunt you've not seen for several years. The conversation ebbs and flows but Lucy never lets it flag.

Over in the converted cinema I ran amok among the endless loaded shelves. Hopelessly addicted to reading from an early age, I lost myself in other people's lives for several hours. Wandering into the medical section, curiosity got the better of me when I found a volume intriguingly titled *Oral Anatomy*. It turned out to be full of gruesome colour plates of diseased mouths which once—so he claims—inspired Francis Bacon. It made me wonder why on earth anybody ever becomes a dentist.

Driving back up to Hays Bluff high above the town, I gave a lift to Phil, a young guy of about eighteen. I had met quite a few young people like him over the previous few months: quiet, shy, and somehow disconnected from the sweeping social changes of the 'eighties. They did not have the innate survival instincts and toughness, the easy camaraderie and gimlet-eyed shrewdness of the young veterans I had met at Stonehenge earlier in the year. Nor did they belong to the Yuppie Wannabees and Flitterati of the kind you find infesting Stoke Newington or Soho (Motto: you are what you say you are, babe). Young and not so young people who devote their lives to the frantic pursuit of trivia.

Phil, of course, was delighted with Pugwash. People like him always are. There is something about Pugs' user-friendly style and unstoppable clowning that opens them up and gets them chattering. If they only knew.

That evening the wind dropped and overhead the last of the hang gliders drifted soundlessly off the Bluff and circled overhead like great birds of prey. The silence was so acute that the whirring wings of actual passing birds was startling. While Pugs admired himself in one of the van's side mirrors—a favourite occupation—I picked some magic mushrooms.

It was cold now and snow showers were forecast for the nearby Brecons. The mushrooms tasted like—well, mushrooms. I went for a long walk to the top of the two thousand foot bluff and, taking in the panoramic views that stretched for thirty miles or more, waited for something to happen. What happened was my feet went numb, the sky turned red, and it started to go all dark. In other words, sunset. Ah well.

Back in the van I had the usual tussle with Pugs for the duvet—and lost as usual—before finally drifting off. And then I had the strangest dream. I dreamed the van was surrounded by giant breasts with erect nipples. I made the mistake of panicking and running out of the van. I immediately found myself surrounded by gigantic homicidal mammary glands. What a way to go! As they closed in, there was a distant sound of wailing and the gnashing of teeth. Over the brow of the hill, several huge orifices appeared and immediately moved in to attack the giant breasts.

This was ridiculous. Apart from anything else, I'm a Jungian. The breasts formed a circle, South African laager style, with nipples facing outwards. I was trapped in the middle. The orifices closed in. Suddenly a hang glider appeared overhead. Suspended below it was Pugwash. He swept down and I leaped to catch his tail. I was carried above the great rearing breasts and over the orifices. Pugs looked down and winked. And promptly dropped me. I fell, twirling like an autumn leaf towards a great yawning orifice—and jumped awake. I switched on the light and Pugwash looked up at me blearily.

'Thanks a bunch, you,' I said to the suitably bemused Pugs.

In the cold light of dawn, a light frost covered the grass. Pugs had already got his shaggy winter coat. It was time, I thought, to be finally heading for home, although there would be one more journey to make—to a certain 'fridge somewhere north of Watford.

Driving down from the Welsh mountains, a lateral thought made a sudden connection between flying reindeer and a particular wind-blown cat. I glanced at Pugs suspiciously. 'You haven't been eating any mushrooms by any chance, have you?' I asked. Pugs stared ahead through the windscreen with a faraway look in his eyes. I wonder about that cat sometimes.

Pugwash had already got his shaggy winter coat.

16
The Ghost of a Chancer

Arriving in Brockley, I found the miniature world of feline reprobates apparently unchanged. Cheesy, the cat world's answer to the haemorrhoid, was draped over the dustbin in a familiar pose. In fact, judging by the state of her, she hadn't moved since April. Wally wandered over, as lopsided as ever, but treble his previous size. A fat Wally? Later I discovered several people in the square—unbeknown to each other—had adopted him since my flying visit in August. Good luck, kid.

I am of little faith. But I tell you: the portents of those few days of my brief stopover in the Great Wen, before my final journey north, were not to be ignored. Killer winds, a Stock Exchange ravaged by Bears, and other wondrous sights—all, I felt, were trying to tell us something. What exactly, I left to higher beings.

As I drove north and east into the rising sun of a perfect late October morning, I consulted the Oracle—conveniently seated next to me washing the remains of breakfast off his face. Having travelled the length and breadth of England over the previous seven months there was only one question to ask, really.

'What the hell is happening to this country, Pugwash?'

Pugs, who clearly regards himself as a Higher Being, and is certainly a member of one of the most successful species of small mammals ever produced by a frail planet, yawned, stretched, and enthusiastically scratched for fleas. Alas. If only I could have interpreted such signs, life would no doubt have all fallen into place like a big jigsaw. But the veil failed to lift, although Pugwash might if he went on scattering fleas about like that.

I was heading for a place just beyond Rotherham, called Greasbrough. Not for the first time, I wondered who it was thought

As I drove north and east into the rising sun, I consulted the Oracle—conveniently seated next to me washing the remains of breakfast off his face.

up the names of northern towns. The motorway was virtually empty and raised above the nearby fields. Frost hollows were still filled with freezing mist and the chill morning air sharpened the autumn colours. It was all right; and the recent domestic news had been particularly cheering. London apparently now had a monopoly on weather, along with everything else. And after the great wind came the great share crash (snigger). I imagined London streets to be full of pedestrianised Yuppies in green Hunter wellies and Barbour coats, wandering about looking vainly for trees to hang themselves from (chortle). Meanwhile, telephone lines in the City were jammed with people getting crossed wires or numbers unobtainable as they desperately tried to unload their Telecom shares (choke). The Unities, as Aristotle might have noted, were being observed.

Certainly on the night of the *Great Storm*—London increasingly perceives itself in italics these days—there was an appreciable pattern to the spectacular chaos. As with the death of Kennedy, Londoners afterwards all remembered exactly where they had been and what they had been doing. Sleeping mainly, and entirely unprepared by and large; thanks to the Met. Office. Brockley was no exception. I awoke at two-thirty in the morning to a steady, consistent roar. Vague memories of faulty plumbing got me out of bed. Opening the kitchen window for a breath of fresh air nearly put me back in one for a very long time. I suddenly found myself pinned against a wall opposite the window and festooned in rubbish: not an entirely new experience in Brockley, although one that usually occurs out on the street around closing time. As I struggled to close the window a thought occurred. This was no ordinary breeze.

Of course the obvious thing to do was to go back to bed. I resisted good sense and a few minutes later found myself leaning into a hurricane. The wind maintained its steady thundering roar as the temperature rose and fell dramatically amid the battle of the Warm and Cold Fronts. Cold won. Icy rain sliced horizontally across the square in front of the house, under a sky black with millions of premature autumn leaves. All around and at regular intervals old, weak or just plain unlucky trees gave up the unequal struggle and crashed to the ground. And suddenly, across the square, appeared an old man with a little dog. We approached each other in slow motion; like two of those white-faced mime artists who invariably appear at left wing benefits. 'Just like the Blitz,' he said excitedly on arrival. I took his word for it. As we stood there in the eye of the storm I wondered, not for the first time, why the English are half in love with chaos while opposing it resolutely with a much admired but frankly misguided stoicism.

'Not a problem you have, is it, kid?' I said to my travelling companion as he gazed stoically out of the van window at the chaos of the (once again) single lane M1.

Soon it was time to turn off. Passing rapidly through Greasbrough —I defy you to do otherwise—I climbed a long hill. I was looking for Barbot Hall Farm and the Barbot taxidermist studio of Graeham Teasdale. Suddenly I was into a minuscule green belt and there by the side of the road was a big hoarding announcing the studio—with the logo of a squirrel (gulp).

The studio was a large out-building of the farm which has been worked by the Teasdales for several generations. The thirteenth-century farmhouse with its eighteenth-century extensions is the oldest building in the area. Perched on top of the hill between the two encroaching towns that never existed for most of its life, it is now under siege from both sides and the final two hundred acres are gradually being whittled away by local authorities.

It was to this tiny, diminishing rural sanctuary that I'd sent the last mortal remains of Podey. Not for the first time, I was experiencing a few qualms over an impulse decision.

As Mr Teasdale went to fetch his son Graeham, I entered the barnlike studio stuffed (sorry) with the tools of his trade. Centre stage was a large table and placed exactly in the middle of it was . . . Whaaaa! Now you have to bear in mind that although I remembered Podey very well indeed—for nearly twenty years we had stood shoulder to ankle against life's slings and arrows—the last time I had seen her she had been, well, dead. And things rarely appear deader than a dead cat. Particularly one that has been run over.

And that was another thing. Then, she had been distinctly banjo-shaped and with (understandably) an amazed expression on her face. Now, she sat on a little plastic pavement in the middle of the table still (understandably) with an amazed expression but somehow —alive! I involuntarily called out, 'Podey?' although God knows what I'd have done if she'd responded. Granted it was close to Hallowe'en, but this was ridiculous. Clearly Graeham Teasdale was a master craftsman.

He appeared: youthful looking, bearded, and with an intense, faraway look behind the glasses that visionaries are supposed to have and his friendly northern voice belied. A few minutes' conversation confirmed first impressions. Graeham was not only an outstanding taxidermist, he was a man with a mission. My impulse decision to renovate a dead moggy had led me into a complex world that seemed at first sight to belong to the past. Like the farm itself, I had assumed taxidermy was on its way out. I was wrong.

Unemployment in the North and Yuppies in the South are two

major factors in its new growth, so I suppose taxidermy can be seen as an unlikely beneficiary of Thatcher's Britain. Somehow, it seems appropriate. Naturally, cowboys abound and that's where Graeham and the guild's mission come in. To the professional, taxidermy is an art form, a branch of sculpture, and looking at the eerily lifelike form of old Podey, I for one was not inclined to disagree.

And how was it achieved? (Skip this bit if you've having breakfast.) Take one dead cat. Skin it and tan—not cure—the hide. Put to one side. Dispose of cat's body. Model cat's new form in clay—which is where the art comes in. Make a fibre-glass piece mould from this and cast in polyurethane foam. (Sorry, Podey.) Stretch the skin of the cat over the cast and secure with pins. Put aside in a temperate place for one month to dry. Finish off cat by modelling highlights of face and fur. And finally, mount the cat (now, now).

I decided to take a photograph of the animate Pugwash next to his

She sat on a little plastic pavement in the middle of the table still (understandably) with an amazed expression but somehow—alive!

renovated old playmate. Pugs strolled in, as laid back as ever—and did a double-take at Podey that was worthy of Buster Keaton. Cats rarely make scorch marks but I think this one managed it as he zoomed across the farmyard and beyond into the surrounding fields.

Two hours later there was still no sign of him, and I was due in Hull for a meeting. Another hour and I was in Hull *sans* both cats.

Later that evening, driving back along the mistbound motorway to Greasbrough, retribution set in. I began to see cat-shaped holes in the shifting grey mass ahead. Guilt was playing a little visit in a not unfamiliar guise.

'How could you?' said a small, stiff, creaky voice like old ice.

'I'm sorry.'

'After all we've been through together.'

'All right.'

'And Pugs is probably lying in the corner of some foreign field, all stiff and cold.'

'That'll make two of you, then . . . I'm sorry. I didn't mean that.'

And so on, as guilt and irritation warred across a tired and emotional mind. I crossed a deserted, ghostly Rotherham and finally arrived at the farm. Silence. A heavy frost silvered the grass. Where to start? I wound down the window.

'Pu . . .' I began and a familiar shape sailed through the window, landed on the seat, curled up, and promptly went to sleep. Relief promptly turned to rage.

'I have just driven! . . . fog! . . . frost! . . . knackered! . . . put one claw wrong, tampon head, and you're the other half of bookends! Right?' Pugwash curled a paw over his ear and slept the dreamless sleep of the truly innocent.

The next morning I collected the Renovated One and headed for the South and Brockley. Nearing London, we began the familiar M1 crawl. Pugs sat nonchalantly next to Podey watching the world go by. At one point we found ourselves beside a coach full of hardened football fans. As I slowly moved past them, the entire coachload gazed across at the dynamic duo in stunned disbelief. They'd probably blame it on the ale.

Several cats, including the main trio, appeared from nowhere.

Back home, everything seemed normal. I entered the house.

Well, the roof was still on. And all the windows were intact. I placed Podey on the mantelpiece and turned on the gas fire. Several cats—including the main trio—appeared from nowhere as usual and collapsed in front of the fire like so many rag dolls. Come hurricane, flood, attacks by wild bears, whatever—nothing could shift this lot. I noticed that Pugwash was deferred to and given the main cat's place nearest the fire. Quite right, too. This was a cat with great tales to tell over the dark winter nights to come. Everybody pointedly ignored Podey, which was probably fine by her anyway. She never did give a bugger what anybody thought. And suddenly I was very very glad to be home.

It felt as if I'd been travelling for a long time. Longer certainly than seven months. And looking back, it seemed a long time for the country as well.

The situation had changed as I travelled, and with it the mood of the country. A nervy resignation had set in, but frustration and sullen resentment were never far below the surface. Particularly with the young. Too many times I had crossed the road late at night to avoid coiled-tight teenagers with clenched fists and thousand-yard stares. In some places, small town centres—peaceful during the day—became no-go areas for a while around closing time.

Meanwhile London had continued on its downward amoral spiral with the ever more cynical Haves continuing to feed their ever-increasing, ever changing needs: any qualms kept at bay by God knows what crawling out of the woodwork and setting themselves up as apologists for their topsy-turvy values. And of course the North-South divide had become a tangible barrier.

'We'll need a passport soon,' the unquenchable Tassie Hamilton had said in Bridlington. The difference in house prices took care of that little detail. But if the mood of the country was deeply troubled and insecure outside London, and suitably grotesque within, never a day went by during my travels without meeting any number of people who turned such generalisations on their heads.

Anyway. I felt both tired and relaxed. I looked at the semi-circle of battered fur sprawled around the fire and overlooked by the immaculately renovated Podey, glassy eyes shining out in the firelight. I've always admired cats. Now I envied them, with their perfect ability to adapt and remain independent at the same time. As I glanced idly around the room at the few familiar objects my ex-wife had left—presumably she'd had trouble getting the wallpaper off—I felt myself sliding into a well-earned sleep.

Well, the old battered settee with the leaking cushion still looked as comfortable as ever. Almost time for the news. More fun on the Stock Exchange, hopefully. I reached over to where the television used to be . . . USED TO BE! Shit! Robbed *again*?

A few minutes later I managed to get through to the local cop shop. 'Hello, Mr Harrison,' said the familiar voice of the police sergeant. 'We've been reading about you.'

It was probably those magic mushrooms.

'Well, what's gone this time?'

I began the litany. As I ran through the items, I looked at the semi-circle around the fire. Warm, fed, contented, unemployable, and entirely at peace with the world. Yes indeed. Cats certainly know something we don't.